PILGRIM IN CHINA

Also by Phyllis Thompson
Freely Given
To the Heart of the City
The Gideons
An Unquenchable Flame
Mister Leprosy
✓ The Rainbow or the Thunder
China: The Reluctant Exodus
Capturing Voices
✓ Minka and Margaret
Within a Yard of Hell
The Midnight Patrol
✓ A London Sparrow
Firebrand of Flanders
Faith by Hearing
Proving God
Matched With His Hour
Dawn Beyond the Andes
✓ God's Adventurer
Climbing on Track
No Bronze Statue
✓ Desert Pilgrim
Beaten Gold
Aflame for Christ
There Came a Day
They Seek a City
Our Resources
Countdown for Peter
Eight of God's Agents
Bible Convoy

Books for children
Teacher Jo Likes Little Cats
King of the Lisu

PILGRIM
IN CHINA

A MEMOIR

Phyllis Thompson

HIGHLAND BOOKS
OVERSEAS MISSIONARY FELLOWSHIP

Printed in Great Britain for
HIGHLAND BOOKS
Broadway House, The Broadway
Crowborough, East Sussex TN6 1BY
by Richard Clay Ltd., Bungay, Suffolk
Typeset by CST, Eastbourne, East Sussex.

CONTENTS

To Irene and Doris
my fellow missionaries
in Siangcheng

1

25 January, 1985

Dear Edward,

As I walked out of the Charing Cross Hotel
with you this afternoon, into the pouring rain, my
heart was singing. And as I sat on the bus that was
to take me back to Newington Green, on the border of Hackney, where I've lived for nearly a quarter of a century, I could scarcely believe it was true.
I had been commissioned to do the very thing I
most wanted to do, and let off doing what I did not
want to do. I smiled gratefully as we separated
after our talk, put up my umbrella, and set off for
home.

You had wanted me to write my own story. You
had mentioned it once or twice and, because I respected your judgment, I hadn't been able to say a
definite 'No!' but the thought of doing it had depressed me. I'd gone to meet you this afternoon
knowing you would broach the subject again and,
sure enough, you did; but I could not come to
terms with the idea. I simply did not want to write
my own story.

Who am I, anyway, that anyone should want to
read it? I'm such an ordinary sort of person, have
achieved so little, started no flourishing Christian

work, performed no acts of heroism. True, I went to China as a missionary in 1936, was there during the Sino-Japanese war, and eventually withdrew, along with all the other missionaries, in 1951, when Communist pressure became too strong for us to stay. True, the experiences of those years have coloured my whole life, which, without them, would have probably taken a very dull course. But there was nothing exceptional about them, nothing to justify me writing a book about myself.

Besides, it would be so boring a task for me. The best part of writing a book, from my point of view, is the research involved, and the interesting people it brings one in touch with. I'm not a creative writer, and inspiration comes to me through other people, not from within myself.

All this I tried to explain to you as we sat drinking coffee in the spacious, comfortable lounge. You looked slightly surprised when I said I'd find it boring to write about myself, and suggested, 'But it wouldn't have to be so much about yourself, as the way God has dealt with you, the way He has led you, provided for you. . .'

Even that did not stir me. After all, every Christian has a story to tell along those lines, so why me? And after about half an hour I said, 'I'm sorry, Edward. If I believed God wanted me to do it, of course I'd do it, even if I did find it boring. But I just haven't any urge in my own heart; no word from Him either.' Then I added, 'I'll tell you what I'd like to do. I'd like to have a shot at writing the story of Madame Guyon.'

A rather resigned expression passed across your face, and you said, 'All right. You go ahead. If that's how you feel I think you should go ahead and do it.'

I knew it wasn't what you wanted, wasn't what you had hoped would be the outcome of our interview. As my literary agent, you'd had quite a different idea. But you said, 'Go ahead,' and when I said, 'What? Write it first, without a contract, then see if anyone wants it?' your answer sent my spirits soaring.

'Oh, I'll be able to get a contract,' you said airily, and mentioned a couple of publishers right away. 'And if they don't want it, Highland—my own publishing firm—will do it.' So I knew it would be all right. It seemed too good to be true. To be able to do the very thing I most wanted to do, and to be assured of a publisher! Sitting on that bus I felt so grateful, so happy, that I had quite a sense of release about writing my own story.

'I'll have a go at it, just out of gratitude,' I thought. 'But I'll do it in a different sort of way—just writing letters, as memories come to me. Then, when I've finished, I'll let Edward see them. If they are any good, then he can go ahead and get them published. If not, no harm will have been done.'

One thing you had said when you were still trying to persuade me to write my own story had encouraged me. It was: 'It would start with your call to China, wouldn't it? What happened before that doesn't really matter.'

But some of what happened before matters very much. So I'll start in the year 1933.

No need to go into those first twenty-six years of my life, with their pleasure-seeking and the misfiring of love affairs: when the young men I could have liked, didn't like me and those who did, I didn't like. The only time when feelings were mutual was in the little correspondence school of journalism where I was working, in Adam Street, off the Strand. My senior colleague and I fell in love with each other and I went through all the traumas and heart-rendings of being in love with a married man.

If I'd been living then in the climate of the present day, I am sure the affair would have gone much farther than in fact it did. What a merciful deterrent to immorality was public opinion! To have been co-respondent in a divorce case would have brought shame on a respectable tradesman's family; to the credit of the man concerned, it must be said that he never tried to persuade me to take that step. The upshot of it all was that he found himself heading for a nervous breakdown, we agreed that we must separate, and I left the office.

But all that was in the past by the spring of 1933. My father was prospering in business and had bought another shop, this time in Andover in Hampshire, and we had moved there as a family of four—father, mother, sister, brother. We got on very well together and had our congenial circles of friends. My own life consisted of dances, bridge-parties, cinemas and smoking, with novel reading to fill in the empty days and hours when there was nothing else on. We played tennis, too, thought I didn't much enjoy it. I wasn't any good at the game but of course I had to play, to keep in with the right people.

It must have been hard for my father sometimes —he had stopped playing cards, drinking and smoking, and went to church regularly when he wasn't out preaching himself in some of the little country chapels around Andover. He always cycled to those little chapels. He wouldn't take the car on Sundays, for fear people got the impression that he was out joy-riding. As a Christian he didn't want to set a bad example by appearing to desecrate the Sabbath. Standards of the 1930s were very different from those of the 1980s. He had to come back to a drawing room full of smoke, where his family were playing bridge. He would look at us rather reproachfully, but make no further demur; and when he invited a preacher to lunch we always tried to behave ourselves and refrain from levity. More or less.

It was at one of these lunches that things got started for me. My father was the moving spirit in organising periodical meetings in the Town Hall on the subject of prophecy and, on this occasion, the preacher—at one time a missionary in the Far East—was our guest. Now Dad, who rarely spoke to me on religious matters, always tried to persuade me to attend those meetings on prophecy. He had given up trying to get me to church, but a meeting in the Town Hall was different. Sometimes I went, sometimes I didn't. He tried again, very guilefully, at the lunch table.

'Are you coming to the meeting this afternoon, Phyl?' he asked pleasantly. It was an awkward moment for me but, before I could reply, the preacher himself turned to me quickly and said, 'Oh, don't feel you've got to come just because it's me, will you?' He could see I was being trapped, and made the way out.

That did it. I felt he had been sporting. Very

sporting indeed. So I went to the meeting.

What he preached about—what prophecies he mentioned in the Old Testament that were being fulfilled in the present day; whether or not he pointed to the events in the Great War of 1914–18 which led up to the Balfour Declaration with its promise of a national home for the Jews in Palestine—I do not remember. I had heard a great deal about it all before: and how it was all part of the divine plan leading up to the culmination of the ages. It was not only the fulfilment of prophecies in the present that interested me, but also speculations as to how prophecies would be fulfilled in the future. Peering into the future had its attractions and was the main reason, apart from wanting to satisfy my father, for my going to those meetings at all.

There was probably nothing very different about what the preacher said that day from what I had heard already. They had all asserted that the consummation of all these prophecies, and the end of world history, would be the return of Jesus Christ to this earth. I'd heard all that before—but this time it had a slightly alarming effect on me. For the first time it dawned on me that this thing was really going to happen. The words I had repeated automatically in the Creed on the rare occasions I had attended church—'. . . and He shall come again with glory, to judge both the quick and the dead'—meant what they said. Jesus Christ was coming back.

And I knew I wasn't ready to meet Him.

I had had no intention of attending the evening meeting, for I had another engagement—one to which I had been looking forward rather eagerly. A group of us had arranged to motor over to the neighbouring town of Salisbury and go to the cinema there, then stop off on the way back for a meal in a café. It so happened that, at that particular period, two young men—one a farmer and the other a teacher—had been showing an interest in me. My natural vanity was flattered, and I had been playing them off against each other. Both were to be in the group going to Salisbury that evening, and since the one for whom I had a secret preference had shown signs of retiring from the field, I was anxious to meet him again and do what I could to revive his flagging hopes.

But the impact of that afternoon meeting was so strong that I felt I could not go off to the cinema in Salisbury.

'I'm really sorry, Charlie,' I said to the young man who had come to take me.'I can't come after all. It's been such a wonderful meeting. I don't know how to explain it—but I just can't come to Salisbury this evening. I *must* go to the evening meeting.' So the young man, docile though disappointed, went off without me.

I've wondered sometimes what would have happened if I had crushed that new sense of awareness of God and had gone off to enjoy the pleasures of the outing. The first stirrings of life are indefinable, and easily ground down—but how much depends on them! I am very thankful that I made the right choice, and went to the evening meeting instead. Not that anything spectacular happened—I just came away with the awed realisation that I'd have to stand before Jesus Christ one day, and that I'd better try to improve myself.

My efforts along that line were rather half-hearted. Worldly pleasures would have to go, I thought, so I cut down on some of them, but not on those I liked the best, such as ball-room dancing. Dancing was my passion—the waltz, the fox-trot, the lancers, the tango. I did not stop going to dances, when I had the opportunity. Yet underneath it all was this vague awareness of God, and of coming Judgment. I started to pray, adding little personal petitions to the set forms I recited by my bedside at night as we had been brought up to do. The empty formality of 'saying my prayers' at any rate had one virtue—it provided a sort of sanctuary in which to commence a search for God.

'Oh, God, give me faith,' was one of those personal prayers, for somewhere I had heard that faith was a necessary ingredient if I was to be ready to face Jesus Christ. I had also heard something of the doctrine of predestination, and wondered whether I was not predestined to be saved; whether I was one of those for ever outside the circle of God's elect. However, that did not worry me overmuch. It seemed reasonable to pray that if I were, if He had not chosen me, He would make an exception in my case and take me in. I did not start attending church, but I did undertake to do the secretarial work for an evangelistic campaign that was being planned in Andover. I thought that was a pretty good thing to do and would weigh in my favour.

Meanwhile, the date for the next meeting in the Town Hall on the subject of prophecy and the second coming of Christ was fixed, and the time was drawing near. I was looking forward to it with a strange feeling of anticipation. I felt that would be the day when something of great portent would happen. I did not know what it would be, but it was as though I was coming up to a crisis; as though I was going to have my one chance of being saved. I'd heard the phrase used, and took it to be a dramatic experience that made one feel entirely different.

The first Wednesday of May dawned. There was no question this time as to whether I would attend the meetings. I wanted to. I went to the afternoon meeting with a keen expectancy of what would occur. Perhaps it would be a vision, a voice, a revelation given to me. I listened eagerly, waiting.

But nothing happened. The speaker—a gentle, courteous, typical Anglican clergyman of the old school—said nothing that specially enlightened me, though at one point in his talk he quoted a short sentence of Scripture with such an expression of rapture on his face that it brought tears to my eyes.

'And the King of glory shall come in,' he said, and momentarily it was as though he had been transported and was actually seeing that King of glory. I caught my breath. For the first time in my life I realised that God is a person, a Being to draw out the affection and loyalty and devotion of the heart. I wished I knew God as that man on the platform knew him.

When the meeting was over my father took the speaker and two other men back to his office over the shop, for tea. I went along too—to pour tea and act the hostess, as my mother wasn't around. I sat there in my smart little fur jacket, with my well-coiffured hair, listening to them as they talked. Then, looking at the clergyman to whom I had only just been introduced, the thought came to me: 'That man will think I'm a Christian—and I'm not!' And because I did not want to be a hypocrite, I butted into their conversation with the explanation which I thought would make clear my position, and at the same time satisfy him: 'I'm not saved— but I'm trying to be!'

There was a sudden silence in the room. My father and his two friends who knew me slightly, stopped talking, though one of them leant forward as though he wanted to speak. But something restrained him. Perhaps Someone restrained him. And the gentle, courteous clergyman looked across at me with surprise and said earnestly, 'Oh, don't try! It's all been done for you.'

It was my turn to look surprised. Don't try! But I thought that was just what I had to do. Try to improve myself, try to be religious, try to be a better person.

The clergyman saw that I was mystified, and said with a smile, 'If your father gave you a horse, or a car, what would you do?'

Well, the horse made no appeal, for I didn't ride. But to have a car of my own would be a different matter. My father had one, my mother had one, my brother had one, but when I wanted to use a car I had to borrow one of theirs. A car of my own?

'Oh, I'd make whoopee!' I said promptly. It is doubtful whether the clergyman knew the meaning of the current slang 'making whoopee', but he got the idea and continued, 'You'd take it and enjoy it, wouldn't you?'

'I certainly would!' I answered.

Then he spoke the sentence that I can only say

was the opening of the Kingdom of God for me. I've repeated it over and over again through the years that have passed since then, passing on the message as it was given to me that day. Just one simple sentence. This is what it was: 'Jesus Christ died on the cross to give you everlasting life, and all you have to do is accept it.'

I stared at him. Everlasting life *given*? All I had to do was to accept it?

I am sure I must have heard the same message before if not the same words but it had never meant anything. This time it was different—like suddenly hearing one's own name at the end of an announcement over a public address system. This time, it was addressed to me personally. I was being told that what I had been trying to obtain by my own efforts and sacrifices was being offered to me for nothing . . . if I would take it.

That same evening, alone in my bedroom, I faced the issue. If I accepted that gift of everlasting life, whatever it might be, it would certainly mean letting go of something. Looking back over the years to what I realise now was the greatest crisis in my life, I am amazed at how almost casually I regarded it, at how little I understood of what was involved. I was just conscious that an indefinable, other-worldly glow had appeared over the horizon of my life, and that I was being drawn towards it; but to reach it I had to leave something behind. Vaguely I realised that this was my old way of life, my ill-defined ambitions to have a good time. I would have to relinquish what I knew for what I did not, leaving behind the familiar for the unknown. So I thought about it for a while. I was not at all sure I wanted to take the plunge: it seemed like diving off at the deep end, into nothingness.

In the end I decided that I'd take the risk. It was not the fear of hell that brought me to that decision, but the feeling that if I didn't take the plunge, I'd be missing the best. Whatever the consequences might be, I'd accept that gift of everlasting life. So down I went on my knees, down went my head on the bed, and I prayed.

'Oh, God, I do accept Thy gift of everlasting life,' I murmured—and waited for something to happen. Nothing did, so, thinking I might not have done it in quite the right way, I prayed again: 'Lord Jesus, come into my heart.' I'd heard that sentence somewhere, and it seemed appropriate for the occasion. Still nothing happened; so, rather mystified, I prayed a third time: 'Oh, God, I do have faith. . .' Then, since there seemed nothing else to do, I undressed, got into bed and went to sleep.

Next morning I woke up, as usual, feeling no different, but with the thought at the back of my mind: 'I must be saved! I don't feel as though I am, but I did what that man told me to do. I accepted the gift.' I went around doing the usual things, but now and then the thought would come again: 'I must be saved. I accepted the gift, like that man told me to.'

That afternoon my mother had a few of her friends in to play bridge. There were five of them altogether so they took turns in sitting out. During the course of the afternoon, I wandered into the drawing room and went and sat beside Mrs. Watson, whose turn it was to wait while the others played. She was sitting on the window seat, overlooking our terraced garden with the tennis court below. I joined her and she turned to me with a smile. After the usual preliminaries, she started talking about the state of the world, about the things that were happening in Germany (it was 1933—the year when Hitler was coming into power) and about what was worrying her most of all—the threat of another war.

'It would be terrible,' she said. 'Poison gas, and that sort of thing. We'd all have to go underground and live in cellars ... food out of tins. . .' She enumerated a few more horrors that she had read about somewhere, then suddenly she turned to me and said, 'What do you think is going to happen, Phyllis?'

And I knew my moment had come.

So suddenly and unannounced come the opportunities of life at times. Swift and fleeting, they have to be grasped without premeditation, or they are gone and nothing can bring them back. It was so in the drawing room that warm afternoon in May. I knew I had to say something about what I believed, right there and then, and the bridge-players intent on their game could nevertheless not fail to hear what I said.

I swallowed hard, then said in a clear voice, 'I believe that Jesus Christ is coming back again.'

My mother told me weeks later that I might just as well have dropped a bomb on that game of bridge. Nobody made any comment, but they started playing wild, trumping their partner's tricks and so on. Phyllis—talking about Jesus Christ! Whatever had happened?

Well, something had happened at last. It had

happened to me. Not a light from heaven, or a breathtaking revelation, or anything spectacular or dramatic. But as I had said those words, there had come into my heart the quiet, unshakeable conviction that I was saved—saved for eternity. I'd been struggling to believe it all the morning; now there was no more struggle. I *knew*. I suppose it is what is referred to in one of the epistles as being 'sealed with the Holy Spirit of promise'. I knew that the gift of everlasting life had indeed been given to and received by me; that I possessed it; that I was born again—a child of God for ever.

Less than twenty-four hours had passed since the man had said those unforgettable words: 'Jesus Christ died on the cross to give you everlasting life, and all you've got to do is to accept it.' I sometimes refer to this as my 'overnight conversion' and no doubt there were some who thought it was too quick, that it would not last. But it has lasted for fifty-one years—that deep, unshakeable inner conviction that I have everlasting life. And fifty-one years is quite a long time.

Well, that's the story without which my call to China would never have taken place; the story of the complete turn-about in my life, which got me facing in an entirely different direction and setting out on my spiritual pilgrimage. Having got it down, I can turn to what I really want to do—research into the life of that remarkable Frenchwoman who lived nearly three hundred years ago, whose spiritual journey into the love of God has inspired so many, including me—Madame Jeanne de la Mothe Guyon.

2

Dear Edward,

A couple of weeks after my conversation with you in the Charing Cross Hotel I met a friend at the National Art Gallery for a brief get-together, not having seen her for about six months. As we sat in the restaurant over our lunch she asked me what I was doing now, and I told her I was starting on another book.

'What's it to be this time?' she asked and when I said, 'The Life of Madame Guyon,' an expression of mingled delight and amazement passed over her face. She looked at me with her eyes wide open and exclaimed, 'Oh! How wonderful. She's my favourite character!'

This was new to me—I'd wondered whether, like so many other people, she would never even have heard of Madame Guyon. But she was the second person to react similarly when I'd mentioned what I hoped to write: 'Madame Guyon! She's been a great inspiration to me. What a worthwhile assignment!' So now I asked my friend what it was about Madame Guyon's story that had so impressed her, and she answered thoughtfully, 'Well, somehow I was able to relate to her. My experiences haven't

21

been anything like hers, of course, but it was her sufferings, and what she learned through them. . . Yes, somehow I was able to relate to her.'

And this is what I am finding as I research into her life again, starting with the book which was written over a century ago, and is still being printed —*The Life of Madame Guyon* by T.C. Upham. Although she lived three hundred years ago, I find some of my own spiritual experiences, and my reactions to them, are just like hers. I can identify, for example, with the fact that immediately after the revelation that came to her through the simple words of a hermit monk, which she always referred to as her conversion she made a clean cut with the amusements and entertainments of the world in which she lived.

'I bade farewell for ever to assemblies which I had visited, to plays and diversions, dancing, unprofitable walks, and parties of pleasure,' she wrote. 'The amusements and pleasures so much prized and esteemed by the world, now appeared to me dull and insipid—so much so, that I wondered how I ever could have enjoyed them.'

I can't honestly say that I cut out dancing, bridge-playing, cinema-going and smoking, primarily because they seemed dull and insipid, but because I saw, from the example of my own father's life, that such things weren't compatible with being a disciple of Jesus Christ. I wanted to be a disciple of Jesus Christ, so I just cut them out. I've always been glad I did it then, in the first flush of that first love—it might not have been so easy later on. As it was, I really had no special difficulty about it—the desire for those amusements seemed to

have died. I do remember passing the cinema in
Andover to which I had so often gone, thinking to
myself, 'I shall never go in there again,' and feeling
rather strange about it. As I walked on, conscious
that a certain activity had been withdrawn, I found
myself thinking, 'I wonder what Christians *do*?'
How did they occupy themselves when they
weren't at church or praying or preaching or reading the Bible?

I've never had occasion to ask myself the question again. Even at that time I found myself well
occupied because, having agreed to act as secretary
for the forthcoming evangelistic campaign, I was
fully involved with making arrangements, writing
letters, getting leaflets printed—all under my
father's direction; and when the meetings commenced, I attended every one for the whole
month.

Two vivid memories of those early months stand
out. The first was the occasion when I took my
mother and two friends to Salisbury, to attend
another of those meetings on prophecy which had
had so great an influence on me. The speaker that
day was a friendly, animated little Jew, named
Mark Kagan, who had become a Christian and who
could speak with authority about the inner meaning of the Old Testament writings. At the end of
his talk, he pressed home the implication of his
message that Jesus Christ was coming back one
day, and invited any present who had not already
done so to ask Him to be their Saviour and to sig-
nify openly that they meant to do so by standing
up, right where they were. In the hush that followed his words two people stood to their feet—the

two friends who had come with me. Contrary to my hopes, my mother didn't join them, though she was rather quiet as she drove us back to Andover. But when we both arrived home she said without any explanation, in quite a matter of fact voice, 'I'm going to put off that bridge party tomorrow—I'll tell them I won't be coming. I'm going to give up bridge for the time being.' Then she added, 'I think we'll burn those packs of cards—we don't want to have them in the house.'

So she went to the drawer and pulled them out —all thirteen packs of playing cards, and took them out to the field adjoining our garden where we lit a bonfire and scattered the cards on it. They did not burn very easily and, while we were pushing them on to the flames, my father arrived home from business. Seeing us in the field, he walked through the gate to greet us. When his eyes fell on the bonfire, he stood there speechless, his face rather white, his eyes very blue. His wife as well as his daughter destroying their playing cards!

'I'm giving up cards for the time being,' announced my mother. It was as far as she would go then. She did not commit herself rashly. But before very long something had been added to the windscreen of her little Austin Seven. It was a text: 'Christ Jesus came into the world to save sinners.' She had taken her stand at last, and she didn't mind who knew it. She never referred to that experience as her conversion

'I came back to the Lord,' was the way she explained it later. She'd come to the Lord, she said, when she was a girl, in a small Methodist chapel in Cornwall. On the whole, there has been little

enough to show for it in the intervening years—
and soon she was deeply regretting this. Then one
day, reading her Bible, she came to the words, 'I
will make up to you the years that the locusts have
eaten.' This was to happen in a way she little expected; in a way that was to call for a greater re-
nunciation than she had ever known. But neither
she nor I had any intimation of that the day we
burned the cards. It was just a step we felt we ought
to take, and we took it.

The other incident that stands out very vividly in
my memory concerns only me, and I remember it
because it involved me in doing one of the most
difficult things I have ever done in my life.

My mother and I had heard about a little group
of people who studied the Bible, preached the
Gospel, and held prayer meetings in a wooden hall
that they had built in a side street—built it with
money and materials that came in 'by faith' we were
told. It was not until we had been attending their
meetings for weeks that we learned that they belonged to the Brethren. That did not convey anything to us: it was the first we had heard of the
Brethren. All we knew was that the local group
were very earnest and were self-governing, with
four 'elders' to run their affairs. One was a jobbing
builder, one a road sweeper, one a shop assistant,
and one a tradesman's delivery man. From time to
time they went out into the market square in front
of the Town Hall and held open air meetings,
carrying long poles with texts painted on banners;
and it was this courageous witness that impressed
me. To go out into the open like that! However did
they feel, and however did they have the pluck to

do it? It was something I felt I could never do. But, as the weeks went by, there came a most uncomfortable feeling in my heart that I ought to make an open witness like that, too. I kept remembering one of the sermons which the evangelist in the evangelistic campaign had preached, using as his text the words, 'And they came to Kadesh Barnea'.

The text referred to the time in the history of the Israelites when they had escaped from Egypt, crossed the Red Sea and, having travelled for some time through the wilderness, had come to the very border of the Promised Land, to a place called Kadesh Barnea. It was at this point that twelve men had been sent to spy out conditions in the land, ten of whom had returned with such an adverse report of the strength and size of the inhabitants that the Israelites had taken fright and refused to go in and claim what God had promised them. The outcome had been that they were condemned to wander for forty years in the wilderness, instead of entering into the land that 'flowed with milk and honey'. The point of the sermon had been that in our spiritual pilgrimage we come to a time when we are faced with an opportunity and a challenge which, if our faith and obedience fail, may result in our remaining in a spiritual wilderness, perhaps for years, perhaps for a lifetime. It had been a solemnising warning.

One evening, praying at my bedside, I was completely convinced that I'd come to my Kadesh Barnea. I either had to carry that banner or wander in a spiritual wilderness for maybe forty years; the latter, I remember thinking, would bring me to the age of sixty-six. I had to do something about carrying that banner, and I must do it soon. The Brethren, I knew, were planning to have an open air meeting in front of the Town Hall in about ten days' time. I could have joined them and, with their moral support, carrying the banner would not have been so difficult; but I felt that I simply could not live through those ten days with the ordeal hanging over me. It had to be now, or my courage would fail and it might be never. This was my Kadesh Barnea.

So the following morning, I went to the elder who was the shop-assistant and who, I knew, kept the banners and poles at the back of the shop where he was employed, told him what I wanted to do, and asked for a pole and a text banner. What text did I want? I did not know—it didn't seem to matter—but I chose, 'Believe on the Lord Jesus Christ and thou shalt be saved.' He did not say much, but I was conscious of his sympathy as he placed the strap over my shoulders, fixed the pole with the banner into the socket at my waist and held open the side door for me to emerge with it into the High Street.

I did not know which way to turn, nor did I know where I ought to walk. To walk on the pavement would impede pedestrians; to walk in the road would impede the traffic. I ended up walking along in the gutter. Up the High Street, past our shop towards the church at the top of the hill, I went, my eyes looking straight ahead with what I hoped was a beatified expression, while feeling as though I was on the way to the stake. It so happened that my father, who often left the window-dressing to one of his assistants, was himself dressing the window that day and, glancing out, he saw his only daughter—grim-faced and carrying a banner— slowly pass by.

This gave him a horrible shock. He did not wait to see me turn round outside the church and walk back. He hurried up to his office and knelt down and tried to pray. He probably thought I was getting what was known as 'religious mania'; perhaps he was not the only one to think that.

'Oh, Phyl, did you really feel you ought to do it?' he asked me later.

'Yes,' I said firmly. 'I had to do it. I knew I'd never go on if I didn't do it.' I had no exultant feeling, none of the inward joy I had expected after making such an effort—quite the reverse. I was emotionally drained and it was some time before I recovered my equilibrium. But I have never once regretted taking that step. I had burned my bridges. There was no turning back now, even if I'd wanted to. And I'd been obedient to what I believed God had been telling me to do. There might be some horrifying battles ahead but at any rate I wouldn't have to spend forty years in the wilderness.

3

24 February, 1985

Dear Edward,

I know that the main reason why you feel my story will be of interest is because of my China experiences. As you said, there are now so few people who knew China in the days before the Communist take-over there, that reminiscences about that period will soon cease altogether. And since China and the Chinese—particularly the Chinese—seem to be written in my heart, I'm only too glad to hurry on with my story until I get there. However, there are one or two things that really must be told if the story is to reveal the deep happenings, rather than the merely superficial ones; for without those deeper happenings I'd never have got to China at all.

The first one was a convention for the deepening of the spiritual life which I attended at a conference centre near Bournemouth. It had been organised by the Japan Evangelistic Band, and I went there on my own, feeling rather strange and very lonely. The convention was over-booked, so I had to be accommodated outside, in a private home occupied by a freelance evangelist and his American wife, Mr. and Mrs. Dunne. I had meals at the conference centre and attended all the meetings there, so did not see a great deal of my host and hostess; but they were very kind to me, and I had some talks with them during which I admitted my private fear that I would not be able to stay the course as a Christian and would become what I had heard referred to as a 'backslider'. I've no doubt they explained many things to me, all of which I have forgotten, but one thing Mr. Dunne said has remained with me to this day. It was a simple sentence of seven words.

'It all depends on your prayer life.' I've found that to be true. Without the cultivation of an inner devotional life, the heart soon becomes unsatisfied and deterioration sets in.

The theme of the convention was really along similar lines, emphasising the inner rather than the outer Christian life, and it was here that I became aware of something lacking in my spiritual experience. I cannot remember any of the sermons, only the continual reference to the Holy Spirit and to what some called 'the second blessing' and others spoke of as 'sanctification by faith'.

'I don't care what you call it!' asserted one speaker vehemently. 'The thing is—have you got it?'

I was uncomfortably aware that, whatever it was, I hadn't got it.

It was encouraging to learn, from what the various speakers said, that there had been a time when they, too, had been aware that they hadn't got it. One man admitted that he had been a Christian for ten years before he realised he was lacking the inner power that he recognised in some others whom he met and started to seek it for himself.

'Ten years!' I said to myself. 'Why, I've only been converted a few months, and I'm seeking it! I must be getting on pretty well.' I could almost feel a sort of puffing up inside until the thought came, 'That's pride! Spiritual pride. And pride is sin.' So I started talking to myself.

'You've got nothing to be proud of. You may have been converted only a few months, and be getting on much quicker than other people, but you've got nothing to be proud of.' I tried to talk myself out of it. 'I will not be proud! Pride is sin.' But try as I would, that puffed up feeling remained. My mind was in a whirl, overladen already with teaching I hadn't heard before, with the emphasis on faith and obedience, victory over sin, a clean heart, power in service. I wanted it all but now there was this unexpected problem in my own heart. I was proud. I had spiritual pride. I'd heard about it and I'd got it and, argue with myself as I would, I couldn't crush it. It was there, and nothing I said would budge it. I couldn't expect this second blessing, this entire sanctification, this filling of the Holy Spirit, whatever it was that others had got and I hadn't, if I had spiritual pride.

As I have said, I was lonely, not knowing anyone at the convention; and in any case, I never found it easy to talk about my problems, though I was quick enough to tell the story of my conversion. That was all very clearcut in my mind and, without wishing to denigrate myself unduly, I realise now that I probably enjoyed the interest aroused. But it was one thing to tell how Jesus Christ had changed my

manner of life, given me a new purpose for living
and a consciousness of eternity, and quite another
to admit that I had an uneasy feeling something
wasn't right. And to tell another human being that
I was feeling very proud of my spiritual progress
would be too embarrassing. So there I was, walking
along the pleasant residential roads of South-
bourne, battling with myself until I got to the point
when I could battle no more.

Then it was that a strange little memory came to
my assistance. I had heard or read somewhere that
the favourite Bible verse of King George the Fifth
was, 'If we confess our sins, He is faithful and just
to forgive us our sins, and cleanse us from all unrighteousness.'

'If we *confess*. . .' That meant coming out with it,
admitting it.

I was at the end of my tether. There was nothing
left but to try this last resource. If it didn't work, I
was finished; I'd have to go on with that secret
pride all my life. There was very little hope in my
heart that it would work, but I'd try it anyway. So
still walking along, I cried out inwardly: 'Oh, God,
I confess. I'm proud. I've got this pride, this spiritual pride, and I can't do anything about it. Lord, it
says that if we confess, You will forgive and cleanse.
Well, Lord, I confess.'

It was almost defiant, that cry. It wasn't what I
would have termed the prayer of faith at all. The
prayer of faith, I thought, was a calm, confident,
unemotional committal of something to God, with
the absolute assurance that He now had it in hand.
That cry of mine wasn't like that. I may have heard
the phrase, 'Let go and let God,' but as far as I was

concerned at that moment I was just letting go. I really had very little confidence that God was at the other end, so to speak. I was too mentally exhausted to care what happened then. If God wasn't able to deal with that pride of mine, there was nothing more that I could do about it.

But God *was* able. I had only walked a few steps when I came to the corner of the road. There, quite suddenly, I stood stock still. It was as though I was being bathed in a sort of warm glow, descending on me from above; and, in some mysterious way which I cannot explain, I was conscious that the pride had gone. It simply was not there. I could scarcely believe it.

I suppose it was what might be termed a mystical experience, of which I have had very few. And, of course, I don't wish to imply that pride never reared its head again—far from it. But that particular form of spiritual pride was gone and I went to bed that night tired out, but at rest. It was a very definite sort of experience, and reassuring.

But I soon realised that it was not what I was seeking—that inner empowering that gave victory over sin, and fruitfulness in service. I knew I still hadn't got it, and I kept on praying that God would give it to me. And the more I prayed, the more depressed I became.

Depressed is perhaps not the right word. It was something deeper than merely feeling low-spirited. It was as though there was something in my heart that was hiding there—some evil which I could not define. I could not understand it. Those people at the convention had been so free, so happy, so un-inhibited; they had spoken so convincingly about the Holy Spirit's presence in their lives, and about the fact that He was God's free gift—'Repent and be baptised, and ye shall receive the gift of the Holy Spirit'—and so on. Well, I had repented, and I had been baptised (that had taken place in a village stream, near Andover, shortly after I had carried the banner) so I seemed to have fulfilled all the regulations. But where was the gift of the Holy Spirit? Instead of liberty, there was an awful sense of bondage; instead of joy, a feeling of guilt; instead of effectiveness in service, there was no evidence of influencing anyone. So what was wrong? I was getting more and more miserable, though I managed to put on an outward show of normality while wondering how much longer I could go on like that.

One day, weighted down with the heaviness on my spirit, I went to my room and threw myself on my knees. Then, as I knelt there in silence, the awful realisation came upon me that I did not love God at all—that, in fact, that evil thing hidden in my heart was a hatred of God.

I was horrified. I'd thought I was a good disciple of Jesus Christ, that I loved Him; but here, hidden in my heart but now revealed, was a bitter enmity against Him. This was something far, far worse than that spiritual pride. Hatred of God! I don't think I knew at that time the verse in one of Paul's epistles when he speaks about the natural heart being at enmity with God. I did not realise that that enmity is inherent in all of us—I thought I was the only one, and I was really terrified. I knew, from previous experience, that there was only one thing to do about this—to confess it. But how could I confess such a thing? How could I possibly kneel there and tell God I hated Him? I can remember it now—the feeling of deep alarm. I knew there was nothing for it! I couldn't conquer this feeling myself, it had to come out; but I really wondered if I would be blasted out of existence if I did it.

So there I knelt, and told God that I was very, very sorry, but I couldn't do anything about it myself—I simply had to confess that in my heart was a hatred of Him.

What happened then was very quiet and unsensational, for I heard no voice, I saw no vision; but the memory of it has remained until this day. It was a sort of revelation, I suppose. I don't know how else to describe it. It was as though I saw a beastly, leering old man, mincing affectedly along, but somehow dressed up to look like Christ. And I knew that that was my Self. My religious Self. Self that wanted to be admired, adulated; that beastly, leering Self; the Self that was at enmity with God.

Then I saw Christ on the cross. No, I didn't really see Him: it was no vision, just a sort of revelation. And I realised what it meant. Christ had taken that sinful Self of mine, on the cross: 'Our old man is crucified with Him. . .'

It was all very quiet and unsensational. I had no overwhelming sense of peace, or joy, or praise, or anything. All I knew was that the sense of guilt had gone.

Around that time, I heard of a doctrine called 'sinless perfection'. I realise now that I had completely misunderstood the teaching. As I understood it then, sinless perfection was a state into which one could almost leap if only one's faith were strong enough—a state in which one never said, thought or did a thing wrong. I thought it was just a matter of having a strong enough faith, and clung to the idea with tenacity, assuring myself repetitively, 'I do not sin, I cannot sin, I am free from sin.' However, I had to give up that idea after about a day and a half. Honesty compelled me to admit that however well it worked for others, it simply was not operating properly as far as I was concerned. What I did find later on, was that although Phyllis Thompson was very much alive, with her desires and her lusts, she could be put in her place by being reckoned dead. So if she was dead, it didn't matter if she was overlooked, or laughed at, or denied natural satisfaction. The effectiveness of Paul's arguments in Romans chapter six is an open secret, hinging on the words, 'Reckon ye also yourselves to be dead unto sin and but alive to God through Jesus Christ our Lord'. I found it only worked when I reckoned.

But still there remained this conscious lack of the Holy Spirit. The sense of guilt had gone, but where was this empowering of the Holy Spirit that I had heard about and longed for? I prayed, I waited in silence, I tried to exercise faith to believe that I'd received it, I did everything I knew, but still there was that deep sense of emptiness, and I was beginning to feel that I couldn't go on without some energising force within.

Then the day came when again I realised what was meant by living by faith. I was due to go to speak at a little meeting for children, and as I descended the stairs that afternoon I felt suddenly afraid. How dare I go to speak for God without the

Holy Spirit? It would surely be presumption. I wished I could call the whole thing off, but it was too late to do that. Then, as I reached the bottom of the stairs and stood in the hall trying to brace myself for what lay ahead, my eyes fell on a little book that had been left on the hall table.

I picked it up automatically, scarcely noticing what it was, and opened it at random. My eyes fell on a text which had been placed under a chapter heading. This is what I read: 'What things soever ye desire, when ye pray, believe that ye receive them, and ye shall have them.'

'Desire' was the operative word, as far as I was concerned, in that sentence. Desire! By this time my whole being seemed to be craving for that inner spring of life, for something that would satisfy a thirst which I could not describe. Desire!

I knelt down there in the hall and prayed as I'd prayed several times before, asking God to give me His Holy Spirit. Then I got up and went to the meeting.

Nothing happened. I was expecting a sort of effulgent glow, or perhaps a feeling of tremendous power as I spoke, but the meeting went off quite calmly, and I returned home reminding myself that what the verse said was that if I believed, I would receive. In the days that followed I sometimes found myself asking again for the Holy Spirit, then pulling myself up with the reminder that I had received, for I had prayed with desire. Then, gradually, I stopped worrying about the matter and the craving which I couldn't describe ceased. I couldn't have explained how or why, but I was satisfied.

It was about a month or so later that it began to dawn on me that there was a difference in the reactions of the children in those little meetings I had started. Previously they had been friendly and responsive enough to me as a person, but what I said about Jesus had apparently left them unmoved. Now there was a change. They listened eagerly, they wanted to pray, they were sorry when they knew they had done wrong. Some of them stayed behind to ask Jesus into their hearts. It was all very unspectacular, but to me it was the quiet outward evidence that I had received what I had prayed for.

Not long after that, I knew I must go to China.

4

8 May, 1985

Dear Edward,

As I look back over my life, and particularly over the early days after I became a Christian, I realise to some extent how great an influence books have had on me. In fact, I think they've made a greater impact on me than sermons, of which fewer than half a dozen stand out in my memory. But books! There is one in particular which directed the whole course of my life, to a country I'd had no interest in before—China.

The book was given to me by Miss Tasker—a middle-aged spinster who lived in a large house in a little village called Anna Valley, about a couple of miles from Andover. A stream ran along at the bottom of her wide, rambling garden, and it was in that stream that I had been baptised, along with one or two others who were connected with the local Mission Hall. Miss Tasker invited me to speak at the drawing room meeting she held in her home from time to time, and generally took an interest in me—this Andover girl who had had rather a dramatic change in her life. She can have had no idea of the effect that her casual little gift of a book would have on me.

9

It was called *Something Happened*, and was written by three women missionaries of whom I had never heard—Mildred Cable and Eva and Francesca French. They had become rather famous in the 1930s through their exploits in the far away region of the Gobi Desert, on the borders of China and Mongolia; but I knew nothing about that. I accepted the book with due gratitude and, having nothing special to do one afternoon, settled down to read it.

I was alone in the room and read on and on, absolutely spellbound. The book took me to a realm I had scarcely known existed, and among people of whom I had never heard; and I saw, through the eyes of those three women, the people of north-west China, the dwellers in the remote oases, the Chinese, the Mongolians, the Tibetans, and the Muslims of central Asia.

I saw, too, the little beggar children, with their sticks to beat off the dogs, and their begging bowls. The story of one of them in particular touched me, for she was deaf and dumb, so didn't hear the dogs barking, and sometimes they were on her, biting her skinny legs, before she could ward them off. (The Trio, as they were called, eventually adopted her.) I thought of the happy, well-fed children who came to my little meetings, and compared their lot with hers. And she represented so many other children, away there in China, who had never heard of the Good Shepherd and never would hear, if someone didn't go and tell them.

I read on—about the people these women missionaries met and the conversations they held, as well as about the disasters that overtook them personally. Once one of them scalded her arm and leg, and there was nowhere to tend her except the cart in which they were travelling, through a dust storm that had blown up.

One incident moved me especially. They had been selling Gospels and Bibles during the day, but in the cool of the evening they went for a stroll round the little houses and caravanserai and booths in that oasis away in the desert. As they walked round, they noticed a man standing by a flare, reading aloud, with a group of other men squatting around him, listening intently. The three women quietly drew near and saw he was holding in his hand one of the Gospels they had sold earlier in the day. The story he was reading was the story of the prodigal son.

As I mentioned, the name of the book I was reading was *Something Happened*; and something happened in me that warm afternoon in a drawing room in a Hampshire market town. Compassion such as I had never felt before filled my heart; compassion for those little beggar children who knew nothing of the Good Shepherd and for those desert dwellers who would never know there was hope for the prodigal if someone did not go and tell them. I always refer to that experience as being my call to China, but actually it was not so much a call as a divine impulse. I heard no voice, I saw no vision; I just felt that deep compassion in my heart, and found myself kneeling beside my chair, praying.

It was one of the shortest prayers of my life.

'Oh, God! For Christ's sake, send me to them!' That was all I said. But I knew God had heard.

5

Dear Edward,

The London City Mission is celebrating its 150th anniversary this year, and as the author of the book *To the Heart of the City*, which briefly tells its story, I have to appear on the platform of the Central Hall, Westminster, to answer a few questions about it. I shall be glad when my part is over. I don't enjoy these public appearances. However, the thought of it has had the effect of stirring my memory.

I have been vividly reminded of the first time I ever stood on that platform, nearly fifty years ago, as one of the missionary recruits of the China Inland Mission, who were very shortly to sail for that country. There were about sixteen of us altogether, mostly women, and it was arranged that each of us should say something about ourselves, in one sentence.

In one sentence! How we girls talked about it, tried over our sentences, prayed most earnestly that we would say the right thing! The prospect of saying something loud enough for everyone to hear (there were no microphones on platforms in those days), without stumbling, and without going beyond a sentence, scared us more than the thought of going to China. Like all the others, I prayed very earnestly that I would know what words I should speak, and eventually I had those words really impressed on my mind, so that at least I was in no doubt as to what I had to say. I can remember it to this day. When my turn came, I stood up, conscious that the eyes of two or three thousand people were focused on me, and found myself saying, 'I must. . .' For a moment I stopped —overcome with stage fright, I suppose—but then I pulled myself together, and said firmly, 'I must work the works of Him that sent me, while it is day. The night cometh, when no man can work.'

That really summed up the sense of urgency which impelled me then and, in a way, still impels me today.

It was the year 1936, nearly two years after I had had the experience in the drawing room at home, when I knew I must go to China. What a different world we lived in then to the one we live in today! I was in my mid-twenties, yet still living at home with my parents, with no thought of moving into a flat and making a career for myself. I was just like the other girls in our set. We lived at home until we got married. If we didn't get married, we went on living at home. It occurred to very few of us to launch out and do something different. So when I told my parents that I thought of going to China as a missionary, it was like exposing them to an electric shock.

I'd been thinking about it for some time before actually broaching the subject, and I did it one evening when the three of us were sitting around the fire, and my mother had apparently dropped off to sleep. I don't remember what my father and I were chatting about, but I do remember saying, 'I feel that God is calling me to go to China.'

My mother sat up with a start. Suddenly she was wide awake, and without any hesitation said, 'I could never let you go!' And she meant it. It is an interesting reflection on the climate of those days that her unwillingness to let me go was an insuperable barrier to my going. It did not seriously occur to me to take a step in direct opposition to the expressed wishes of my parents (my father maintained silence on the subject, though I knew that he would not stand in my way): in any case the China Inland Mission, to which I had thought of applying, would not have accepted me: at that time it was against their policy to accept a young woman whose parents were actively opposed to her joining them and going to China. So there was nothing for me to do but to wait. Looking back I am surprised at the equanimity with which I did so—and also at the quiet conviction that I would go to China, and that I had better do what I could to prepare myself for what I'd be likely to do when I got there.

What would I be likely to do there, anyway? I wasn't a nurse, and I wasn't a teacher so, as far as I could see, the only thing I'd be able to do would be to go to remote villages and preach the Gospel from house to house. In order to get some practice in that sort of activity, I determined to go once a week to Charlton, a village about a couple of miles from Andover, and go from house to house, and preach the Gospel.

Whether it was that I was just plain scared of

doing it alone, or whether I felt it would be good to encourage others to do the same thing, I don't know. Perhaps it was a combination of both. At any rate, I enlisted the help of some of the children who came to the meetings I'd started for them and who had given evidence of coming to faith in the Lord Jesus Christ. There weren't many of them, but they would take turns to come, two at a time, with me on Saturday afternoons to Charlton, give out tracts, and stand by me when I had the opportunity to speak to the people who came to the doors and were willing to listen. So that is what we did.

How satisfactory it would be if, at this point, I could tell of souls converted as the result of this effort, or of some spiritual movement in Charlton; but, as a matter of fact, I know of no such outcome. The children and I went faithfully on Saturday afternoons; we prayed about the people we met; we certainly had a heart-warming sense of fellowship and satisfaction as we trudged back home again. But of the various conversations I had with people in Charlton, I only remember one. It was with an old man who stoutly declared that he had been a believer once, but wasn't any more, and that he had a very low opinion indeed of the people who called themselves Christians. Then he added, surprisingly, 'But I will say that I think more of you than I do of most of them.'

This was gratifying, though it took me aback for a moment. I asked him why. What was it, I wondered, that had won his grudging approval? I was waiting for him to say something about my having made a clean cut from the world, having turned my back on idle pleasures, being diligent about proclaiming God's word, not being ashamed to speak for Christ, or something like that. I was quite unprepared for his answer, and didn't know what to make of it. What he said was: 'Well, you do *care*, don't you?'

Care? Of course I cared. It really mattered to me that people should love God, have their sins forgiven, be born again. Would I go about giving out tracts, and talking about God when I met anybody willing to listen, and be ready to go to the ends of the earth to do so, if I didn't really *believe* what I believed, if I didn't *care*? At the time I took it for granted that I was doing what I was doing because I cared; it didn't occur to me that anyone would do it for any other reason. However, fifty years later I realise a little better what that old man meant. If love for God subsides, love for man subsides too, and that caring quality is lacking from the proclamation.

To return to my story, and how it was that I started in earnest on the road to China. It happened quite suddenly, at a weekend convention which my parents and I attended in the little village of Anna Valley. The speaker at the Sunday afternoon meeting was a missionary from China. In the course of his talk he told a moving story about an old Chinese woman, and her devotion to the Lord. It touched my mother's heart, and there and then she made a vow to the Lord from which she never went back. I knew nothing about it until, a short time later, we were sitting next to each other at the tea table and she said to me, 'I told the Lord this afternoon that if He wanted you in China, I was willing to let you go.'

That was all I needed to know. On my other side sat the Secretary of the China Inland Mission; without a moment's hesitation I turned to him and asked what I had to do to apply to the Mission and go to China.

Less than two months later I was in the Women's Training Home in Aberdeen Park, Highbury, London, and a thoroughly good time I had there. It was my first experience of living a communal life. There I was among a group of other young women in their twenties, also fervently hoping to go to China, and I loved it. Our training for missionary work in China included attending lectures, peeling potatoes, washing up the dishes, and obtaining permission from Miss Bond, who was in charge of us all, if we wanted to be out later than 10 p.m. on Saturday, our free half-day. Strangely enough, none of the restrictions irked me, though I found potato peeling for about twenty people tiring and rather monotonous. I remember on one occasion feeling so strung up after some domestic duty that I thought to myself, 'I'll go and have a good cry when I've finished—it will do me good.' But when I had finished, I looked at my watch and realised that I simply hadn't time for that good cry. Not if I was to be ready for the lectures the next day—there was too much preparation to be done. So I gave up the idea, and went to my desk in the study instead.

Another memory of those days has to do with money. Several of the girls were 'living by faith'—in other words, they had no money of their own, and were learning to trust God alone to supply their needs. Wonderful stories they had to tell from time to time, too—postal orders arriving by post in the nick of time, money being pressed into their hands by friends who had no idea they were down to their last penny, and so on. But I was in a different category: my father continued to give me the allowance he had given me when at home, and that was always sufficient for current expenses; so I really had no opportunity to 'live by faith'. I was not at all sure that I would ever be able to do it, and it worried me a bit, until one day the opportunity came. I was asked to attend a week-end convention somewhere, and when I worked out how much it would cost, I realised I should not have enough to cover expenses.

This was the time to pray to God to send me the money I needed. I must say nothing to anyone about it, just pray. And I felt I must be specific. Having found out what the expenses would be, and how much I would have in hand to meet them, I arrived at the conclusion that I needed ten shillings. So I started to pray each day that the Lord would send me ten shillings. I tried to believe it would happen, but in that fight of faith I felt I was often losing the battle. Never had I received an unexpected gift of money, and why should it come now? And from whom?

The days went by, the week-end convention was drawing nearer, and still the money had not come, and I was beginning to wonder what I would do. It was an unwritten law among us that we never told each other if we were hard up, and although I knew that if I wrote to my parents the money would be forthcoming immediately, I felt it would be a complete failure in faith to do this. I'd asked

God to send me ten shillings and I had to go on believing He would do it.

And, of course, He did it. One day I went up to the bedroom I shared with two other girls and over to my little chest of drawers to get a handkerchief. Opening the top drawer, I saw an envelope with my name on it. Raising my eyebrows in surprise I picked it up and looked at the writing. It was unfamiliar to me. Then I opened the envelope, and drew out its contents.

A bank note for ten shillings. Nothing else. No word of explanation—just the ten shillings. The exact sum I had been asking for.

The sense of awe that came over me as I looked at it comes to me now as I record the incident. It was for me one of the outstanding experiences of that whole year in the Women's Training Home. Even the simple explanation of where the money came from, which I learned later, could not diminish the awed wonder with which I received that ten shillings. A benevolent friend of the Mission had decided to give a gift of ten shillings to each of the girls in the Training Home, so all received the same sum at the same time. But to none of them did it mean what it meant to me. I was learning to live by faith not only in the spiritual but also in the practical sense.

The months passed, with their round of lectures, study, prayer meetings, household chores and practical experience in evangelism which meant going, trembling inwardly, to speak at meetings or visit with experienced people from door to door. All the time the thought of going to China loomed in the background of our minds, with the uncertainty as to whether, after all, the London Council of the Mission would accept us. We had been accepted for training, but it was understood that at the end of that period, if we were considered unsuitable, we could go no farther. As the dreaded day when we must appear, one by one, before that august body, drew nearer, most of the candidates were in a state of tension, but I was surprisingly calm. There was a reason for this. I had been reading some of the books written by Amy Carmichael of Dohnavur in India and had been so moved by them, so drawn to the work she was doing in rescuing little girls from a life of prostitution in the temples of India, that I almost hoped the London Council would turn me down. In that case, I decided, I would apply to Dohnavur. I went in to face the solemn assembly of men sitting round the boardroom table, who were to interview me, feeling almost jaunty.

However, they did not turn me down, although they accepted me on unusual terms. I could go out to China as a member of the China Inland Mission on the condition that my father paid for my support. I expect that at the age of 29, with no academic qualifications except a rather sketchy period in journalism, and with only a couple of years Christian experience, I was considered too uncertain a quantity to justify an unconditional acceptance, especially as my medical report wasn't too satisfactory. The doctor had said I was anaemic and highly strung. I might not stay the course, might need to come home before I'd finished the first term of service. Whatever the Council's reason, that was the condition of acceptance.

Looking back, I am surprised that it never occurred to me that my parents might not agree to it. They might well have decided that if the Mission was not prepared to accept me as a normal responsibility, it probably meant that I was not really equipped for a missionary career on the other side of the world. However, the thought never seemed to have occurred to them, either. As I travelled back to Andover in the train from Waterloo that day, it was with the assurance that I had been accepted for China, and my parents, who met me at the station, heard the news as though they had been expecting it. God had called me to China, they both seemed to recognise that, and of course they would provide the financial support for their only daughter! I asked that it should be paid into the General Fund of the Mission, not ear-marked for me personally, because I wanted to be just like everyone else, and if funds were low, as quite often happened, and a normal remittance could not be paid, I'd be in the same position as the others. That was arranged and to all intents and purposes I was an ordinary member of the China Inland Mission, not in the category of the few who were 'self-supporting'. (Incidentally, some years later I slipped into the ordinary membership anyway.)

Written like that it all sounds very practical and matter of fact, but emotionally it was a strange experience of exultation and grief. Looking back over half a century, one realises afresh how rapidly the world has changed, and how the missionary scene has changed, too. There were no 'short termers' in those days. When we joined the China Inland Mission we expected to spend the rest of our lives, until we were too old to work, in China. We would return to our home countries periodically, for a leave, but the terms of service between leaves would be of uncertain duration—possibly a decade or so. The first term of service was the only one with a specified time limit. It was understood that young people who had had to adapt to an entirely new style of life in a strange country with a different climate might, after seven years, get to the point where they needed a break, so then they would be granted leave. So my parents knew they would say goodbye to me for seven years, without any likelihood of seeing me during that time.

Those were the days before universal air travel, of course. The mere sound of an aeroplane was enough to have people stepping out of doors to have a look at it. The very idea of getting to China in a day or two was unthought-of. The quick overland route via Russia and the Trans-Siberian Railway took only about a fortnight, but the usual way was by liner via the Mediterranean and the Suez Canal, the Indian Ocean and round South Asia to Shanghai. It took just over a month. And since, as missionaries, we would be living in the interior, involving journeys by cart for days on end, the geographical separation of thousands of miles, measured in time, could be anything from four weeks to four months. No emergency at either end could bring us together more quickly than that. In fact, when we said goodbye we knew it would be for seven years, with no possibility of meeting before that time.

And we loved each other.

I can remember our parting. We had had lunch

and the maid had brought the coffee tray into the lounge: a daily ritual. So we sat down to drink our last cup of coffee together. But somehow we couldn't get it down.

'I must go!' I said with a sort of gasp and, simultaneously, we all got up. My father ran upstairs. My mother, without a word, helped me get my coat on and collect my bags. My father came downstairs and I saw he had been crying. His eyes were red and, as he hugged me, he half-sobbed, 'I'm sorry, darling. It's just the natural, you know.'

'Just the natural.' Therein lay the grief.

The last glimpse I had of them was walking back from the gate together, towards the house, looking straight before them, my mother's face sternly set.

'They're great, aren't they?' my brother said in a choked voice, as he drove me away to Southampton to join the members of the C.I.M. party on the P. and O. SS Ranchi. It was the greatest sacrifice my parents had ever been called upon to make, and they had made it. I've always felt that in the heavenly records the words that God spoke to Abraham were repeated to them that day. '. . .Now I know that thou fearest God, seeing thou hast not withheld thy son, thine only son, from me. . .' Only in their case it was a daughter.

Therein, in the indefinable way only those who have had the experience can understand, lay the exultation.

We did not say much about it. Feelings were too deep for words. It was costing them more than it was costing me; I knew that. The hardest part was knowing the suffering it caused them—something they tried not to show.

There was a word for me, too. 'He that loveth father or mother more than me is not worthy of me. . .' Well, I was proving I loved Him best, anyway.

At midnight the liner started steaming slowly away from the docks at Southampton. I lay in my bunk looking through the porthole as we passed the lights, one by one, along the quay until at last we were clear of them, and making for the open sea. That was nearly fifty years ago—but I remember it as though it were yesterday.

6

Dear Edward,

It's just a week since I finished writing the last of these letters to you and during that time I've had two quite surprising reminders of China, far away from it as I am now, in London. The first one followed a knock on the front door three days ago. I went to answer it, and there on the doorstep stood a tall, slim, elderly man, smiling diffidently. He knew that 8.30 p.m. was rather late for an unannounced call.

'Christopher!' I exclaimed. 'Come right in! I didn't know you were over here. When did you arrive?' He had emigrated to Australia about twelve years ago, but something draws him back to the old country every year, and I'm one of the people he looks up. Our point of contact is the fact that his parents were missionaries in China and, when on leave, often used to stay with my parents. That was over forty years ago, but my knowledge of Christopher Fairclough stems from what I heard of him then. Christopher, the only child of Mr. and Mrs. Fairclough, was the apple of their eyes and what it must have cost them to sail off for China in the 1920s, leaving him behind in England to finish his schooling, only God knows. I write that reverently. Only He saw the tears shed in the darkness of the night, only He knew the tugging at their heart-strings at the thought of that young schoolboy they had said goodbye to.

'I didn't see my parents for ten years,' Christopher had told me once, and there'd been a catch in his voice as he'd said it, but no tinge of bitterness; and when they'd eventually returned home for retirement, he'd made up for all the times of separation by providing a home for them, living with them, spending most of his spare time with them, right up to the time they'd died. No regrets!

And now, in his seventies, sitting in my lounge, he was happily recounting a trip he had recently made into China, along with about a dozen others of about his own age who had been at school with him in Chefoo: the school in China for missionaries' children. He could tell me all the places they had been to, and stories connected with them. Only one stands out but it is so picturesque I must recount it.

The party had arrived at the very compound where one of its members had lived as a child, somewhere in the vast interior of China. As this person had looked around, he'd suddenly remembered something.

'I used to play hopscotch here,' he'd said. Then he'd continued, 'And I had one special stone that was very easy to kick. I was very careful with that stone, and used to hide it away so no one else could find it. It was under the wall there. . .' and he'd walked over to the spot, put his hand in the hole and exclaimed, 'It's still there! The very stone!'

He'd picked it up and held it in his hand, reminiscently. The recording tape of memory had spun back and stopped to recall a little English boy in the middle of China, playing hopscotch then hiding away his stone

My second visit was from a young Englishman who heard God's call, 'Go for me to China,' through reading *God's Adventurer*, the life of Hudson Taylor that I wrote for teenagers years ago.

He only knew me as the author of the book, so when I told him, in answer to a question, that I had been a missionary in China myself years ago, he wanted to know where I had been. So I got out a huge map of China and pointed to a variety of places before my finger came to rest on the province of Henan.

'This is where I spent my first years in China,' I said. And the tape recorder of memory spun back for me, to the year 1937 when, having completed six months in the language school at Yangchow (where Marco Polo had once been the mandarin), I arrived at my first mission station.

I can see it now, that walled-in compound in the city of Hwaiyang, if I close my eyes and switch off from the present. The way to it led along one of the main streets, with its hard dirt surface (which turned to thick mud when it rained), its dark little open-fronted shops with their merchandise spilling over into the road along which men, women and children, walked or loitered to haggle or gossip, and the occasional, dog, pig or goat made its way. A huge, double-leafed door with the words 'Inland Mission' over it, was all there was to indicate that I had arrived at my destination, that spring of 1937.

My senior missionary, Mr. Jack Tomkinson, had escorted me from the Language School in Yang-chow. I have forgotten every detail of that journey, which took two or three days, but I remember those double-leafed doors and the room that lay immediately behind them, with its two or three rough benches and coloured posters on the wall, and the door-keeper whose job it was to chat to anyone who wandered in from the street, and en-sure that only those with legitimate business got any farther. I was briefly introduced to him, then Mr. Tomkinson led me through the room out along a narrow cobbled path, flanked by a couple of rooms with paper windows which were used for classes on Sundays, and on to the surprising sight of a large courtyard with a shrubbery before a colonial-style house, complete with verandah and balcony and—at right angles to it— a neat little three-roomed bungalow which I was told I would share with Irene Steele. Irene was two years my junior in age but two years my senior in China, which at that stage, counted for much more. We had met in England shortly before she had sailed and, having kept in touch with the occasional letter, were not strangers to one another; but I had never met the Tomkinsons before.

They were a middle-aged, childless Australian couple who could not have been kinder to the thirty-year-old Englishwoman now landed on them to be licked into shape as an 'up-country mission-ary' in agricultural Henan. They did everything they could to help me and make me feel at home. I never remember them once being critical or censorious—not even on the occasion when I and one of the servants had words, and Mrs. Tomkinson had to intervene and mediate.

That incident comes to mind as I am writing, so I'd better be honest and relate it. It provides an interesting glimpse into missionary life in China before the Second World War and, alas, of the faulty character of at least one of the members of a Mission generally esteemed for its piety.

One of the surprises of those early days in China was to find myself in the unaccustomed position of being waited on by servants. I came from a middle class home with one 'maid of all work' and a jobbing gardener but now I found myself in an establishment in which were a gate-keeper, a cook, a goatherd, a water-carrier, a house-maid or two and, in addition to that, a sort of lady's-maid for Irene and me. They were all fairly necessary in the backward conditions of inland China in those days, with no drainage, no electricity or gas, no laid-on water, no milk deliveries, no tinned or packaged foods, no telephone, no motor transport, and several days' journey to the nearest railway. If we had had to do all the marketing, water-carrying, washing and ironing, cooking and vegetable growing, cleaning and grain-grinding ourselves, we should have had no time for the preaching and teaching which we were there to do.

Another reason for employing servants was that it provided work for needy Christians, and this was the case with our lady's maid.

This damsel, an orphan, had been sent to Bible School by well-meaning missionaries but after graduation she had found no opening to work as a

Bible-woman employed by the church, so it had been decided that a job should be given to her with the Tomkinsons' two junior workers. She would do their housework, washing, ironing, mending and shopping, and occasionally accompany them when they sallied forth on a preaching foray if the church Bible-woman was otherwise employed. This was a bit of a let-down for a Bible School graduate who had hoped for a more exalted position; so our lady's-maid was not the easiest person to whom to issue instructions, far less to whom to point out faults. Gentleness and humility were not her outstanding characteristics; nor were they mine, as I discovered to my dismay when I drew her attention to some dust left on my desk. When she flared up angrily, I flared back, angry voices were raised, and Mrs. Tomkinson came across to our little bungalow in consternation to see what it was all about.

'Teacher Dong complains that I haven't dusted her room properly, Madam,' the lady's-maid burst out.

'I did not complain,' I retorted. 'I merely pointed out that there was still some dust on my desk.'

'Teacher Dong licked her finger and drew it across the desk,' continued the lady's-maid, addressing Mrs. Tomkinson, 'Now you know, Madam, that if you lick your finger and draw it across wood, it always looks as though there's some dust there, even if it's just been dusted.'

Indignantly I denied having licked my finger and drawn it across the desk.

'Yes, you did!'

'No, I didn't!'

Anything more childish it would be hard to imagine. Here was a missionary who had come all the way from England to proclaim Christ and His love, going at it hammer and tongs with a young Chinese woman who had graduated from Bible School for the same purpose—all over a little dust on a desk! Mrs. Tomkinson was the one who emerged from the scene with flying colours. How she did it I don't know but she managed to quieten us both down, in such a way as to maintain a primary, if unwritten law in Chinese society, which was that you should never cause someone to 'lose face'. Mrs. Tomkinson sorted things out without either of us feeling that we had lost face.

There is a lot to be said for that law. Granted, it can be abused,—as when it is used to cover up corruption—but the basic principle of showing consideration for another's feelings, of not putting anyone to open shame, makes for good working relations. The maintenance of self respect, which is lost when one loses face, was very important in Chinese life. Mrs. Tomkinson observed that law very adroitly in dealing with her junior worker and the lady's-maid. The matter was closed.

Or so I thought.

But I was wrong.

That night, as I knelt to pray, I found I could not do it. The memory of that brief scene came between me and God. My anger had burst out and, although it had all been smoothed over outwardly, it had not been put right inwardly. I prayed for forgiveness, but no peace came and I knew there was something else that had to be done. It did not need the words in the Sermon on the Mount, about first being reconciled to one's brother before bringing anything to the altar of God, to convince me. It was not just a matter of talking it over with the lady's-maid, pointing out that I hadn't meant to be critical, arguing that she flared up first. Who had started it wasn't the point. As far as I was concerned, I had lost my temper so I had to acknowledge to her that I had been wrong in that.

And that is what I did, the very next day, as soon as there was an opportunity when we were alone together. It was all over in a minute.

'I ought not to have lost my temper with you yesterday,' I said. 'I'm sorry.' She looked surprised then hung her head a little and murmured, 'I ought not to have lost mine, either. . .' We said no more. But I had no difficulty about praying next time I knelt down to do so. The cloud between me and God had been dispersed.

Oh, may no earthborn cloud arise,
To hide Thee from Thy servant's eyes. . .

I've often found that the performance of a simple action, like apologising or paying a debt or putting something right, clears that cloud more effectively than any amount of praying.

Incidentally, the lady's-maid and I got on a lot better together after that.

7

Dear Edward,

Something has happened recently which has radically changed my attitude towards your idea that I should write my own story. As you know, I didn't want to do it, and started writing these letters in quite a casual manner without committing myself to anything. I had no word from the Lord, as I'd told you, so felt quite safe about dilly-dallying.

Well, the word from the Lord has come, so I'm writing straight away to tell you how.

I'd arranged to spend a few days with my friend, Flora Sarpy, who lives in South London, in order that I could get on with writing about Madame Guyon. I was looking forward to it and thought I had brought everything required when, on un-packing, I discovered to my dismay and conster-nation that I'd left behind the very material I needed for the next chapter. Without that material I could do nothing. I stood stock still in that bed-room, overwhelmed with irritation and disappoint-ment, and the more so when the thought came: 'You can't write about Madame Guyon, but you can go on writing your own story.' Just what I did not want to do! But suddenly there was a solemn sense of a Presence in the room, and into my mind the words seemed to flood: *Have not I commanded thee?*

There was no denying the authority behind those words. I saw nothing, heard nothing, but I could not doubt Who had spoken them. I knew what I had to do that day. Rather reluctantly, I admit, I wrote another letter. I'd got myself on the way to China by the time I went to bed that night and I knew that I'd done the right thing. The next day I went home, got the book I needed to continue with Madame Guyon's story, and settled down for another spell of wrestling with the problem of what to include, what to condense, and what to by-pass in her life. And I let the thought of my own story take second place, just writing another letter in a desultory sort of way until I felt rather guilty, and decided I must be absolutely sure about 'the word from the Lord'. I had been quite convinced about it that day a couple of months ago but, like Gideon of old, I wanted tangible confirmation. So I put out my fleece.

'Lord,' I prayed. 'Let me either hear that sentence, or see it somewhere, so that it comes from outside as well as inside. Then I'll know that it is from you, that you want me to finish writing my own story—and I'll obey.'

Well, within three days it happened. I was glancing through the notebook in which I am jotting down extracts for the Madame Guyon story when, to my amazement, I saw written in my own handwriting, 'Have not I commanded thee?' and the date, 9.7.1985, beside it.

There can be no doubt about it now. I'm getting

in touch with you to decide practical details, but from my point of view they are of no great significance. I've had the divine go-ahead, so ahead I will go. As I no longer have any of my China diaries and letters, I'll have to depend on memory—and I find myself wondering what it will come up with.

8

Dear Edward,

Thanks so much for your reply to my last letter: 'I think you should just keep writing and then do a final edit when it is all down. This book can grow as the Lord brings the memories to you. If you had asked me whether you should write a book in this way, I should have said "No." But you have chosen to do so, and it works!'

Yesterday I completed another chapter of the Madame Guyon book, so before settling down to the next one I'm letting my memory slip back again to that mission compound in Henan, China, where I arrived as a new missionary nearly fifty years ago.

Such apparently unimportant things come to mind and how little I remember of what must have been the major events of those days! It was the year 1937, when Japanese troops first invaded China, triggering off the Second World War as we can see now. But at the time, in our quiet compound in central China, we were unaffected by what was happening up in the north, where there had been a shooting-up incident somewhere on the Man-churian border.

The memories that come to mind are isolated

incidents, like the Sunday morning service in which I was sitting among the women on our side of the central aisle, while the men occupied the benches on the other side. (Sex segregation was strictly observed in those days, and we had been instructed time and time again in the Language School that we must never look a man in the eyes when speaking to him. We must address our remarks to the second button on his gown.) And a bird flew in.

On this particular Sunday the congregation was rather sparse and attention was not at all good, either, as Mr. Tomkinson preached on Psalm 84. There seems to be an ebbing and a flowing in most churches, and the ebb was much more evident than the flow in the church in Hwaiyang at that time, what with the Chinese pastor having been seen to observe idolatorous practices at heathen funerals, and Mr. Tomkinson, as missionary-in-charge, finding himself in a difficult position as a result. A complete break with idolatry was incumbent on anyone wanting to become a Christian and join the church; but what did you do when the pastor himself compromised on that point? I did not know the ins and outs of the affair, or what Mr. Tomkinson had said to the pastor and the elders, but I did know that the pastor had prevaricated and taken no steps to rectify the wrong example he had given to his flock. I also knew that he wanted to keep up appearances and had made a public gesture of going up to Mr Tomkinson in a friendly way, and that Mr Tomkinson had turned his back on him. This was a serious matter, for by that action the missionary had made the pastor 'lose face'. Some church members sided with the pastor, saying the missionary was too hard on him, while others took the view that the missionary was doing the right thing. After all, by publicly bowing to the idols, had not the pastor made his Lord lose face? So the atmosphere was thundery, to say the least.

Yet of all the services I attended in that church, the one I remember most clearly was that one when a little bird flew in. It came through the open window soaring up to perch on a rafter in the roof, and Mr. Tomkinson, lifting his arms to point to it, said with a thrill in his voice, 'The sparrow has found a house, and the swallow a nest for herself . . . even thine altars, O Lord of hosts, my King and my God!'

Whenever I read that verse, I see him again— that down-to-earth, practical harrassed Australian —looking up rapturously as though momentarily transported into the realm where he found his security: '. . . even thine altars, O Lord of hosts, my King and my God.'

It is not the only verse that always carries me back to that compound in Hwaiyang. On one occasion, feeling mentally weary from close study of Chinese, too tired to read the Bible and pray as I usually did, I went out into the courtyard and walked over to a little enclosed garden, in which a few gooseberry bushes and raspberry canes fought for survival among the vegetables. Opening the gate, I went in. It was very early in the morning and very quiet. The weather had been dry and hot but, there in the garden, I noticed that everything was drenched in dew. And as I walked round, without a thought in my head, unable to think, far less to pray, the words came quietly to my mind, 'I will be as the dew unto Israel.' As imperceptibly as the dew, falls the dew of God's refreshing peace on the soul. I always think of that little vegetable garden in the early morning when I come to that verse, written nearly three thousand years ago by the prophet Micah.

'He feedeth among the lilies'; that is the third verse which I always associate with my first mission station in China. The words came to me from the Song of Solomon, as I was lying one night in my little bedroom in our small, three-roomed bungalow, looking up at the sky. They reminded me that our relationship to Jesus Christ is not to be one-sided. The Song of Solomon makes that very clear; and the verse about Him feeding among the lilies brought with it the realisation that it brings Him satisfaction when He comes, as it were, into the garden of the soul, and finds it flowering. His first complaint in the messages to the churches in the book of Revelation was: 'Thou hast left thy first love.' And there is something very touching about those words in the second chapter of Jeremiah: 'Thus saith the Lord: I remember thee, the kind-ness of thy youth, the love of thine espousals, when thou wentest after me in the wilderness, in a land that was not sown.'

Perhaps this is a good point at which to try and address the matter you raised when you first sug-gested I should write my autobiography: how I have coped with being single. I have often been asked about this, usually by girls who are learning to cope with the condition themselves. Well, here is my story.

As a little girl, thinking vaguely about the future,

I had the feeling that I would not get married. Not
that it worried me, of course: I was only a little girl;
but every now and then, when saying my prayers at
night, as we were taught to do in those days, I
would add the private and personal plea, 'Oh, God,
give me a good husband!' I mention this because it
has a bearing on what will follow. The Lord did not
answer the prayer to give me a good husband and,
as I went through my late teens and early twenties,
all my involvements with the opposite sex misfired:
either I didn't like them or they didn't like me; or,
as in the one case I mentioned, it was mutual but he
was married and so we separated. So when I was
converted, at the age of twenty-six, I was still single
and my sights were set in another direction. I
wanted to be a disciple of Jesus Christ, come what
may, and as, fortunately for me, I was heart-free
anyhow, singleness presented no problem at the
time.

I don't remember how or when it dawned on me
that it simply was not God's will for me to marry,
but I do know that I became very very sure about
this. At first the realisation was very daunting. The
prospect of going through life alone, without the
comfort and companionship of a husband, was not
an attractive one. But the day came when I knelt
down before the Lord and accepted His decision. I
really *accepted* it. I made no vow, but I suppose it
was the next thing to it. I did pray, very earnestly,
that He would keep from me the temptation and
the opportunity to marry, for I didn't think I'd be
strong enough to keep myself. So that was that. On
one occasion my mother mentioned that I might
marry when I got to China, and I said, 'No—I think

I'm going to plough a lonely furrow.' It quite upset her. Most mothers want their daughters to marry. Fathers, too, for that matter. Mine wrote to me when I was in China and said he was praying that I would get married, and I wrote back post haste, in quite a panic: 'Don't pray for that! I'd be backsliding if I did!' He was thoroughly taken aback! But the conviction was that deep with me, and I have always been thankful for it. Not that it has kept me from the desires and even the strong temptations that come when that inexplicable, powerful attraction sparks off between a man and a woman which we term 'falling in love'. We cannot go through life always shielded from temptations.

'Satan has asked to sift you as wheat,' Jesus said to Peter on the very night in which he later denied knowing Him. 'But I have prayed for you, that your faith may fail not. And when you have turned back, strengthen your brothers.' Those siftings of Satan at least have the salutary effect of making us realise our own weakness, and therein lies our strength; for, as the apostle Paul wrote, 'To keep me from becoming conceited . . . there was given me a thorn in my flesh, a messenger of Satan, to torment me. Three times I pleaded with the Lord to take it away from me. But he said to me, "My grace is sufficient for you, for my power is made perfect in weakness." Therefore I will boast all the more gladly about my weaknesses, so that Christ's power may rest on me.'

The simple secret of being happy, though single, lies I have found, in sublimating, not suppressing, natural desires. As Paul puts it in 1 Corinthians chapter seven, the married woman tries to please her husband, and the single woman tries to please the Lord. Such a positive attitude—deliberately choosing to do the things that will satisfy Him— provides a quiet joy in what might otherwise be tedious or uncongenial service. Brother Lawrence, in *The Practice of the Presence of God*, describes it perfectly when he speaks about doing everything for the love of God.

Not that the married woman doesn't have this attitude, of course. But there are times when she is faced with conflicting loves and loyalties. I remember the occurrence of one such occasion very vividly. I was living for a while on a mission station with a young married couple, and the husband, an ardent evangelist, had been away on a strenuous tour of the outstations. He arrived back early on Sunday morning, having roughed it for several days and all ready to be made a fuss of!

Now Sunday was always a special day for the country Christians, especially the women, many of whom walked in on their little bound feet from the villages around, coming early in order to study their catechisms, ask questions, and share their difficulties. It was the only opportunity they had; and, as—almost without exception—they were illiterate, the hour or two before the service commenced was a very precious time for them. We women missionaries, along with the Bible-woman, always made a point of being free for them then.

On this particular Sunday morning I was there, as usual, fully involved with one and another, answering questions, teaching new characters, listening to confidences. Then, just as the bell was beginning to ring for the service, I hurried back to the house to get something I'd forgotten. Entering the kitchen I gave a start of surprise. There was the wife taking a cake out of the oven! I had not realised till then that she had not been at the front of the compound with the women; and I shall never forget the cloud that came over her face as she looked at me.

'Yes,' she said before I could say a word. 'I know I ought to have been there with the women. . . But Dick wanted a cake. . . So I made him one. . .' I realised that this dilemma—a clash of loyalties—was something I would never have to face; and for that, at least, I could be thankful.

Well, I hope that is sufficient answer to the question, 'How have you coped with being single?' There is, however, just one more privilege connected with the state which to me is the most precious of all.

It is the way the Master went. I am thankful I have been called to follow the same path as He.

9

Dear Edward,

It is surprising how often during the last few days the memory of that secluded compound in the middle of China has come to mind. Even as I sit here writing in my terraced house in Hackney I can see it: the colonial-style house with a couple of old wicker chairs on the verandah; the balcony above looking as though it could do with a fresh coat of paint; the shrubbery in front overgrown and straggly. The place was clean and well swept but rather shabby. Our little three-roomed bungalow was somewhat more presentable, having been redecorated for its new occupants. Previously it had been used as a store-room and, even after the careful planning of Mrs. Tomkinson, was sufficiently frugal to fit in with my idea of what a missionary's manner of life should be. Furnished with a bed, a washstand, a table and a chair and little else, it just suited my ardent desire for simplicity, even hardship in measure. And as my days were mainly taken up with studying Chinese, which I found very tedious, I took satisfaction in the reflection that the room in which I spent so many hours was not unlike the one provided by the Shunammite woman for the prophet Elisha.

Those Biblical personalities, along with many others, became very real to me. However restricted the body may be, the human spirit is free to wander backwards and forwards through time and to enjoy a sense of companionship with those whose experiences bear some resemblance to one's own, though one has never known them in the flesh. This was one of the deepest, though unexpressed, impressions of my years in China. The inevitable sense of isolation felt when surrounded by a people whose language and customs were strange was compensated for by a consciousness of intimacy with many of the human beings whom I met through the pages of the Bible. I wonder if that is what is meant by the assertion we make when we repeat in the Apostles' Creed the words, 'I believe in the communion of saints.'

A consciousness of intimacy developed also with some of the Chinese with whom I was brought into contact in those early, inarticulate days in Hwaiyang. One of these was my language teacher, Mrs. Fan, mother of five. She came along daily—a neat figure in a long gown, as befitted a woman who had received some education, rather than the jacket and trousers of those who had not. She walked on feet that had developed normally, too—another sign of distinction among women back in the 1930s. Foot-binding was supposed to have gone out with the Revolution in the early part of the century but custom dies hard and it was practised widely in the villages, where a girl's beauty was judged as much by the smallness of her feet as by the contour of her face. In any case, once a child's foot had been bound long enough, the malformation was as difficult to rectify as it had been to make. The custom had started in the dim centuries of the past, when an emperor, one of whose wives had run away, decreed that the women of his kingdom should henceforth be for ever prevented from running away from their husbands by having feet too small to run on. Later such feet came to be regarded as an emblem of charm rather than a sign of servitude.

The fact that Mrs. Fan's feet, though small by western standards had been allowed to develop normally, gave evidence that she came of an enlightened family. Apart from that, she resembled the other women in that her dark hair was neatly pulled back into a bun and long trousers were glimpsed through the slits up the sides of her straight gown which buttoned right up to the chin, revealing no part of her person except head and hands. The colour of her clothing, like everyone else's, was blue and, beyond a silver pin in her hair, no jewellery in the way of brooch, necklace or earrings, adorned her. Such things were rarely seen on respectable women on the great plain of central China. The tribal women on the Burmese border might sport their silver ornaments and the bold-eyed Tibetan women their swinging earrings, but the women of the ever-expanding race of Han depended on none of these things to enhance their charm or draw attention to themselves. To my unaccustomed eyes they all looked the same, and we women missionaries did our best to look like them. We, too, dragged our hair back and wore long trousers. Being accepted as belonging to the educated class we wore long gowns rather than short jackets, but the colour was inevitably some shade of blue.

Few of us looked like Chinese, in spite of our efforts. We were the wrong shape; our hair, if not curly, was probably the wrong colour as were our eyes and skin; our very deportment oozed the energy of the West rather than the tranquillity of the East. We were different and, as we were a rare species among the hundreds of millions of inland China, we attracted attention wherever we went. We could always be depended upon to draw a crowd. They came silently and stood simply staring at us, as people years ago must have stood staring at performing bears. For the Chinese woman who was willing to accompany one of us in public, especially before we could understand or speak the language, it must have been rather like leading such an animal around. For those who were instinctively shy and retiring, answering the questions asked about the white-skinned person's sex, age, married status, manner of eating and reason for being there was an ordeal. But it provided them with the opportunity to align themselves with those who had come to preach the Gospel of Jesus Christ, and thus take up the cross in witnessing.

I'm sure it was not without a struggle that Mrs. Fan took on this role. She had been coming daily to my room for several weeks, patiently correcting my pronunciation as I read aloud after her and explaining obscure passages, before I broached the subject of going out to visit and preach the Way. This process of visiting to preach the Way was the accepted method whereby women could proclaim

God's message of salvation without offending recognised standards of decent behaviour. The men could go to the public tea-houses and markets and talk to whoever assembled there, but the women must confine themselves to the domestic scene, addressing themselves to the women sitting on their doorsteps or in their secluded courtyards. The only way I could learn how to do it was by accompanying someone who knew the correct procedure—and who better than Mrs. Fan?

I broached the subject rather diffidently, realising I was asking her to do something beyond the task for which she was employed. She was a steady church member but not noted for her evangelistic zeal, and I wondered how she would react to my suggestion. She was courteous but somewhat reserved as a person, and our conversation until this time had been limited to polite enquiries as to each other's general condition ('Are you quite peaceful?' 'Yes, quite peaceful. Are you also peaceful?') and observations about the meaning of Chinese words. On this occasion, when she understood what I was asking, she hesitated a little, then volunteered for the first time a glimpse into her spiritual life.

'Some time ago I prayed to the Lord that He would give me the opportunity to serve Him,' she said. 'With five children to look after I have not time to do much and I did not know what I could do.' Then she went on, rather slowly, 'I think this is God's answer to my prayer.' It was evidently something she hadn't bargained for—accompanying a white-skinned foreign person through the streets and into compounds, to assist her in proclaiming the Jesus doctrine. With what inward dismay she had received the suggestion she did not divulge, except by the hesitation to respond which I had detected. But she agreed, solemnly. And when I intimated that I realised it would involve a sacrifice on her part she answered, 'You have come all the way from your own country to proclaim the Way. If you have done that, it is a little thing for me to go out with you once a week.'

That brief conversation put our relationship on quite a different level. From that time on we were fellow-workers, and she was as good as her word about accompanying me—clumsy-looking, tongue-tied foreigner that I was—to the homes of local people. She was wise in the way she did it, too. There was no haphazard emerging through our double-leaved front door to meander at random along the narrow street, hoping for an invitation to enter some courtyard or other. When she arrived on the first Saturday her plans were well prepared.

'We are going today to visit Mrs. Chang in the west suburb,' she said. I was rather surprised. Mrs, Chang, neat and thin, was the highly respected woman deaconess in the church in Hwaiyang and, on the face of it, to go and visit her was not my idea of evangelising the heathen. However, as things turned out, there was more to it than a polite, semi-social visit. Arrangements were being made to invite neighbours to meet the new missionary who had come to teach the Way and Mrs. Fan helped me to put into intelligible Chinese a little talk I had prepared, based on an illustrated poster. (In the event, Mrs. Fan did most of the talking, elucidating what I tried to say.)

And so, one Saturday afternoon in the summer

of 1937, I was launched by Mrs. Fan as a preacher of the Gospel in China. Armed with a roll on which was the illustrated poster and a few simple tracts, I walked with her out through the west gate of the city, along the dusty road of the suburb, lined with stalls and tea-shops, and arrived at the gate of Mrs. Chang's compound to find, to my delight, that my best friend was waiting there to receive me.

I'll have to stop there. Changes in my present manner of life are pending, for I have put my house on the market—a process which means, among other things, disposing of most of the furniture and possessions I have accumulated over the quarter of a century I've lived here on the border of Islington and Hackney. 23rd June is the deadline I've set for evacuating the house, and it will be for me a very significant milestone, opening up a new vista for what may well prove to be the last lap of my earthly pilgrimage.

10

26 June, 1986

Dear Edward,

Well, the move has been made, and I am happily settled into the spacious home of my friend, Flora Sarpy. As I walked yesterday from Wandsworth Common station across the well-wooded common with its little lakes, its clumps of gorse and blackberry bushes and its thick waving grass, it did not seem possible that only ten minutes earlier I had been on the busy, bustling London terminus of Victoria. I had commented on the surprisingly countrified atmosphere of the area to a chatty fellow-passenger on the train, and she had asked, 'Do you live there?'

'Yes,' I replied simply. I'd only moved in a couple of days earlier, but I lived there now.

'Lovely garden?'

'Yes.' I thought of the broad, cool lawn, the flower-beds surrounding it, the old apple tree and the laburnum, and the background of trees screening the gardens and houses of neighbours. Yes, it was a lovely garden. I am very content to have reached this Beulah land and ready to continue the long story of how I got here. So back to the gateway of Mrs. Chang's compound, where my best friend was waiting to receive me.

What is a friend? 'One attached to another by esteem and affection,' one of my dictionaries tells me, while an older one puts it this way: 'One joined to another in intimacy and mutual benevolence, independently of sexual or family love.' Both express very well the relationship between Eastern Light and me.

I met him very soon after my arrival in Hwai-yang, when Mrs. Tomkinson started easing me into the work by giving me a Sunday School class of little boys to teach, of whom Eastern Light was the oldest. A rather sentimental little boy he was, with a habit of putting his head on one side and looking sheepish when confronted with some problem that he could not solve or caught out in inattention during the preliminary exercises, yet with a certain sense of dignity, as befitting one who was the eldest grandson of the church deaconess, and the big brother of a brood of smaller brothers and sisters and cousins. From the outset he was a special friend to me for he seemed to recognise and happily appropriate the love I had for my Sunday School class. I really loved those children! Bound as I was by barriers of a language and customs with which I was not familiar, there was little I could do to express it but Eastern Light sensed it and responded. I came to rely on him quite a lot, for he had already heard most of the Bible stories that I told, and was therefore able to translate to the others what I was trying to say. And he had an inborn sense of responsibility for his brothers and sisters. One incident stands out vividly in my memory, for it held an inner significance which has meant a great deal to me ever since.

It occurred during the early exercises of the Sunday School, when all the children were together; the little ones at the front, the older ones at the back. Sitting on the very front row was Eastern Light's little sister—a wide-eyed damsel with two plaits which were braided so tightly that they stuck out at right angles from her head. Her legs dangled from the bench, for they were too short to reach the ground, and after a time, obviously bored with the proceedings, she straightened them out, slid off her seat, and betook herself off. As I watched her depart I wondered if I ought to go and bring her back but decided against it. She would not take the slightest notice of what I said and, short of forcibly bringing her back, arms and legs flaying about and screaming vociferously (I knew the young lady's temperament), my efforts would obviously be fruitless.

However, big brother Eastern Light, sitting some rows behind with the older boys, also saw her. Had it been one of the other little girls he would have ignored her completely, but this one was his sister. He also rose from his seat and walked out quietly but purposefully after her. For a minute or two nothing more was seen of the two children. Then a little figure reappeared in the doorway—a rebellious-looking little girl, dark eyes angry. She returned to her seat and scrambled up on it, defiant still, but obviously having met one whose authority she could not but acknowledge. A moment or two later Eastern Light walked in, too, and resumed his place with the unconscious assurance of one who, after all, has a certain standing which must be respected.

It was at about that time that I had been especially touched by something I had read in the Gospels: 'For whosoever shall do the will of my Father which is in heaven, the same is my brother, and sister, and mother.' It was the word 'sister' that had touched me. To the best of my knowledge and ability I was doing what I believed to be the will of God—and therefore Jesus Christ owned me as His sister. That little incident in the Sunday School in Hwaiyang, nearly fifty years ago, still speaks to me. If I wander off my Elder Brother will exercise His authority and bring me back. He has had to do it, more than once. . .

To return to the meeting in Mrs. Chang's courtyard. Eastern Light had risen to the occasion in a surprising manner. He had invited some of his school friends and it seemed that not for a moment did he forget his responsibility as host. He met me at the gate, bowed politely, and escorted me in. Backless benches had been arranged in the courtyard, and to these benches Eastern Light led his small friends, courteously finding places for them to sit down and afterwards, when it was time for them to go, escorting them to the gate, chatting politely. He and I did not have much opportunity to speak together, but we looked at each other and exchanged smiles occasionally: we understood each other. And how excited we both were when, the following Sunday, two of his school friends accompanied him to church! We looked at each other with the triumphant smiles of fellow-fishermen who have caught something in their net.

Meanwhile, Japan's undeclared war with China

was progressing with alarming velocity. The conquering armies of the invaders were gaining possession of more and more cities on the main railways and roads. News was reaching the Tomkinsons of their advances and it all became suddenly very acute when we heard that the neighbouring city of Taikang had been occupied. Two members of our Mission were stationed there.

'Taikang's gone! Miss Wallis and Mrs. King—I wonder how it is with them!' was Mrs. Tomkinson's immediate reaction to the news. She looked worried. 'Those two ladies alone there!' Her thoughts flew anxiously to her fellow-missionaries. Perhaps, too, she wondered if her husband would be called on to go to their aid and what danger it might lead him into. But he was quite reassuring.

'They'll be all right,' he said confidently. 'They're from a neutral country. We all are: English, American, Australian. . . The Japs are bound to respect us. Our governments are behind us and the Japs know it. They're not looking for trouble. They've got enough on their hands already.'

There seemed no need to be alarmed, although we couldn't help wondering how those two fellow-missionaries of ours were faring. No news came from them, but that was not surprising. If they were in any difficulty they would apply to headquarters in Shanghai for instructions or to the Mission's superintendent in Henan Province, living in Loho.

It was not long before news reached us from the superintendent in Loho. He wrote to say that he intended visiting the two ladies in Taikang, to find out how they were managing in the changed situation and to take them their remittances in cash as it was difficult to get money to them through the usual banking channels now. He would be coming to Hwaiyang on route. Then came the information that one of the ladies, Mrs. King, would shortly be returning to England on furlough. That information was followed by an unexpected suggestion. As Miss Wallis would be left alone it was felt she should have a companion, and that either Miss Steele or Miss Thompson should be re-designated to Taikang.

Mrs. Tomkinson bridled indignantly at that. One of her young junior workers to be exposed to the uncertainties of living in a Japanese-occupied city! Far better that Miss Wallis should come and live in Hwaiyang for a time, until things settled down a bit, she said. It would be so much safer. But, of course, that argument got no farther than the breakfast table, over which the matter was discussed. Personal safety was not a primary consideration. There was a job to do, a responsibility to fulfil, in Taikang. Quite apart from her spiritual work of teaching and preaching, Miss Wallis' presence on the church compound would ensure, as much as was humanly possible, that the place would be inviolate from the incursion of Japanese soldiers. There was no question of her leaving her post. It simply remained to decide whether Miss Steele or Miss Thompson should be appointed to keep her company.

The lot fell on me—probably because I was the older of the two. And so the day came when I emerged from the compound in Hwaiyang, stepped into a rickshaw, and was conveyed out through the city gate, accompanied by Mr. Weller, the Mission Superintendent from Loho, riding a bicycle, and a coolie, pushing a wheelbarrow containing my luggage. We were to pass through the enemy lines to go to Taikang.

Passing through the enemy lines sounds much more dramatic and dangerous than in fact it proved to be. It would have been very difficult to have defined exactly where those lines were. The countryside through which we travelled, with its wheat fields stretching away into the distance and clumps of trees dotted here and there to denote the presence of villages and hamlets, appeared as peaceful as ever. There was not a sign of a soldier, either Chinese or Japanese, nor the slightest evidence of war. The farmers and peasants we passed on the road were going about their business in their usual placid manner; life in the villages continued the same, with hens pecking in the dust, the occasional pig routing in a rubbish heap, children playing in the road, mothers suckling their babies at the doorways of their homes, food vendors sitting beside their stalls.

Yet it was all rather uncanny and there was an indefinable atmosphere of suspense. We were approaching the city that had fallen to the enemy. Enemy soldiers might appear at any moment but in what manner we did not know.

Eventually we saw them. There were three of them and they were evidently off duty, for they were lounging on rough benches at a trestle table outside a little thatched roadside inn, sipping tea. I would not have known that they were not ordinary Chinese soldiers had it not been that the colour of their uniforms was a sort of mustard colour, different from the khaki of the Chinese.

Mr. Weller drew alongside my rickshaw and, cycling beside me, murmured, 'They are Japanese. We'll go straight on.' Silently we drew alongside giving no indication that we had noticed them, although I couldn't refrain from glancing at them out of the corner of my eye to see how they were reacting to the unexpected appearance of Westerners in this remote part of China. They were staring, but made no move to stop us, and we passed by unchallenged.

So we had passed through the lines! As we approached the gate of the walled city of Taikang I wondered what awaited us. Once again, nothing happened. A Japanese soldier was on sentry duty there, but the usual string of coolies was passing imperturbably in and out with their carrying poles swinging across their shoulders or pushing wheelbarrows laden with goods. We, too, passed through unmolested. I learned later that these Japanese garrisons were strung out so thinly along the trade routes and comprised so few men that they usually kept a low profile. They could not afford to take the risk of antagonising the populace unnecessarily.

Taikang, to my unaccustomed eyes, looked much the same as Hwaiyang, with the same dirt roads, alleys of thatched hovels, open-fronted shops and high walls enclosing the compounds of the well-to-do, their large double-leafed gates opened to reveal glimpses of the courtyards within. It was into one of these compounds that we turned, and I found myself in what proved to be a large campus with a church building prominently situated in the front courtyard, and a number of other buildings distributed in courtyards around what was to become the centre of my life for many months—the missionary's compound.

This was more imposing that the one at Hwai-yang and I was duly impressed by the appearance of the two-storeyed house with its wide verandah and balconies as I came on it through the entrance hall. The large courtyard was tidy and well swept, with two or three pomegranate trees in the centre, and low tiled-roofed buildings around it which served as bedrooms for guests.

I was impressed, too, and at first slightly awed, by the lady who was to be my senior missionary. Miss Eva Wallis was stockily built, with wavy grey hair and a fair complexion, and the Chinese gown she wore completely failed to disguise the fact that she was English, through and through. She moved with the calm assurance of one whose undisputed position was that of the mistress of a household. She came forward to meet us just as though we were guests who had arrived for afternoon tea, shook hands politely as Mr. Weller introduced me, and said, 'How do you do, Miss Thompson. I hope you had a good journey? Do come in and have some tea.' Her manner and accent were impeccable.

I felt that I had been suddenly transported back to a London suburb and that an English maid, neatly dressed with cap and apron, would appear at any moment carrying a tray with scones and cream. Such was the atmosphere of calm and security that 'Auntie Eva', as I called her after we'd

known each other for a few weeks, always managed
to convey. No matter what alarming situations
arose, what disturbing rumours were circulated,
Auntie Eva remained the well-educated, matter of
fact Englishwoman who never forgot her manners,
was unabashed by anyone, went about her duties
with unfailing regularity, enjoyed her food which
she ate unhurriedly, and had a robust sense of
humour which revealed itself quite unexpectedly
in seeing the funny side of simple things, rather
like a child. She was completely without guile, and
rose to quite unexpected situations fearlessly, as I
soon observed.

An unexpected situation arose the very night
after our arrival. After supper, Mr. Weller had led
family prayers and then we had all retired to our
respective rooms. Our lights were out, when the
sound of stones alighting one by one on the pavement of the courtyard broke the silence. Then a
man's voice was heard calling our in carefully
enunciated English, 'Mee-sis Wallis! Mee-sis Wallis!
How do you do, Mee-sis Wallis!?'

The patter of stones was resumed, then the voice
called again: 'How do you do, Mee-sis Wallis?'

There was little doubt as to whose voice it was. It
was a Japanese soldier, almost certainly drunk, who
had climbed up on the wall and was trying out his
English. I lay in my bed in one of the guest rooms,
rather apprehensively aware that if he jumped
down from that wall he would be within a few feet
of my bedroom door.

'How do you do, Mee-sis Wallis?'

Then a voice answered him from the balcony of
the house—the rather indignant voice of an

affronted Englishwoman.

'What are you doing, throwing stones into our courtyard in the middle of the night? You are a very rude man. It is very rude to throw stones into other people's courtyards.'

Auntie Eva had appeared on the balcony, arrayed in a dressing gown. I could see her through my window as I lay there in bed and the form of her remonstrance took me so by surprise that I started to giggle. There was something so incongruous about that English voice rebuking the soldier of an invading army as though he were a naughty, impolite schoolboy.

Then another voice was heard, this time from the doorway of the guestroom where Mr. Weller had retired to rest. Mr. Weller was a quiet man, probably rather timid by nature, but he had his wits about him. He realised that only the simplest of sentences would penetrate the understanding of the intruder, so he confined himself to three words, clearly spoken with polite firmness.

'Please go away.'

The whole episode was taking on the form of a comic opera: the deserted courtyard; the only light coming from the lamp held by the female figure on the balcony; the serenading soldier on the wall; the vigilant guardian down below; the 'characters' repeating their lines without moving from their positions.

'How – do – you – do – Mee-sis Wallis?' in broken English.

'Very rude to throw stones into other people's courtyards. . .' in the correct accent of a better-class London suburb.

'Please go away,' in a quiet, masculine voice of authority.

By this time I was under my bedclothes, convulsed with laughter, and wondering who would move first. Eventually the soldier on the wall disappeared, probably dragged down by wiser companions; the figure on the balcony retreated into the room from which it had emerged; the vigilant guardian below turned back to his bed. And no more stones were thrown into the courtyard.

So ended my first night in enemy-occupied territory.

11

26 February, 1987

Dear Edward,

Over two years have passed since I started writing these letters to you and during that time I've written two more books—*Madame Guyon*, which was published last November, and one about the Scripture Gift Mission, the manuscript of which I handed over to Hodder and Stoughton a couple of weeks ago.

I enjoyed that S.G.M. assignment. The research involved took me a number of times to their head-quarters at Victoria and, as I commuted there from Wandsworth Common several times a week, it seemed quite natural for me to be 'going to the office'. That is what I had done in my teens and early twenties, and the routine was familiar. The atmosphere was congenial, too, and the journey home crowned the day, for when I alighted at the station I had to cross the common on which black-berry bushes were laden with fruit, just waiting to be picked. It is quite impossible for me to convey the pleasure I had, day after day, in walking across that picturesque common and picking blackberries. It reminded me of my childhood holidays in the heart of Kent, where we spent a fortnight each year

with Auntie Bessie and Uncle Bill. They lived in a
thatched cottage two or three miles from Lenham,
standing all alone by a winding road among woods
and fields—so different from our semi-detached
house in Ealing. With what excitement did I dance
up and down our compartment in the train as it
slowed down at Lenham, and we saw Uncle Bill in
his corduroys, waiting on the platform to greet us!
Wandsworth Common station has somehow re-
tained its rural appearance, similar to the one I
remember, and in my eightieth year I savoured
afresh the pleasure of those childhood holidays
with their adventurous excursions into the wood,
the feeding of free-range hens with handfuls of
corn flung over the ground, and the picking of
blackberries.

Well, the commuting to the S.G.M. offices is over
now and, as I'm due to meet you in a fortnight's
time to discuss my next book, I must control the
tape recorder of my memory and spin it back—not
to a cottage in Kent but to that missionary compound in Taikang on the vast agricultural plain of
central China.

The months I spent there were unique in my
experience, with one day in particular standing out
as a highlight in my life—a day never to be forgotten, when the angels of God stood by me.

It happened some weeks after my arrival. During that time the Japanese invaders had retreated
and the city had been re-occupied—not by Chinese
Nationalist troops but by Chinese guerillas. I remember how surprised I was to learn that they
were feared far more than were the Japanese.

'But they are your own people!' I exclaimed

when one of the servants was telling me in a voice low with apprehension, that the guerillas had come.

'They are worse than the Japanese,' she murmured, and I was to learn later how ruthless they could be: preying on their own people—torturing some, holding wealthy landlords for ransom, abducting young women. At the time, however, with my very limited understanding of Chinese, I knew little of what went on beyond the walls of our large campus.

I do remember one occasion, when the pastor and a church elder came to see Auntie Eva on behalf of a man they knew. In some way he had fallen foul of the guerillas and, now that they were in control of the city, he was in danger. They were looking for a place where he could hide until he could be smuggled out of the city, and the pastor explained, rather diffidently, that there was only one place they could think of where he would be safe: only one place that even the guerillas would regard as inviolable. That place was the English-woman's private apartment.

They had come to ask if their friend could be hidden in Miss Wallis's bedroom for the night.

Auntie Eva's reaction to that suggestion was prompt and unequivocal. Whether it was the impropriety of the idea or the wiser consideration that she should not get involved in local politics, I do not know; but there was no question as to what she felt about it. She was horrified. A man to be hidden in her bedroom? Certainly not! She wouldn't hear of such a thing!

After they had departed, and we had sat down to

supper, we had a good laugh together as we tried to picture what the Mission authorities in Shanghai would have said if they heard that Miss Wallis of Taikang had had a man under her bed all night.

She was quite firm about not giving asylum anywhere on the compound to men who were on the run, whether from the Japanese, the Chinese Nationalists or the guerillas. As the citizen of a neutral nation living in a country that was at war, she had to be careful to avoid any appearance of partiality, to give no cause for suspicion that she was working for one side or the other. When it came to giving asylum to young girls, however, it was quite another matter. With soldiers about in such troubled times, they were in special danger and parents were only too glad to bring their teen-aged daughters to live in what was considered the safest place in the city of Taikang—the missionary's compound. There were about twenty of these girls accommodated somewhere on the premises and it was their presence that gave Auntie Eva an idea for providing her junior worker with a little experience in preaching.

'You know, Phyllis,' she said one morning at breakfast, 'I think it would be a good thing for you to have a meeting for those girls once a week. It's a good opportunity to teach them the Bible, and nothing is being done about it.'

'Oh, Auntie Eva, I couldn't!' I said in alarm. To be faced by some twenty giggling Chinese school-girls was a very diffrent matter from leading a Sunday School class for four or five little boys. 'My Chinese isn't good enough.'

'Hsiong Ling will help you,' replied Auntie Eva.

Hsiong Ling was a gentle, affectionate girl, who readily agreed to help me run a meeting for the schoolgirls.

This became a regular Tuesday afternoon occurrence on the compound. We taught the children a few choruses and the Lord's Prayer, read a passage from the Bible, repeated—over and over again—the text on which I was to speak, and then I had the ordeal of delivering the sermon.

I took that assignment very seriously. Most of Monday was taken up with praying about it and preparing it. My main concern was to obtain from the Lord the particular message He had for each occasion, and I found that certain verses would be impressed on my mind in such a way that I was assured they were from Him. Usually they were verses that contained some aspect of the message of the Gospel itself, centring on the Lord Jesus Christ, which, of course, presented no difficulty.

However, one Monday the verse that persistently came to mind was different. It came in the familiar words of the Authorised Version, from Psalm 34, verse 7, and I couldn't get away from them: 'The angel of the Lord encampeth round about them that fear Him, and delivereth them.'

Angels. I did not want to draw attention to angels. I believed there were such beings, of course —the Bible referred to them in a number of places—but I did not feel they should be the subject of a sermon to a group of girls who needed to know the way of salvation. I tried to turn my thoughts to a more suitable verse, but I could not do it.

'The angel of the Lord encampeth round about

them that fear Him, and delivereth them.' There was no escaping it. This was the verse I must speak on, so I learned it off by heart in Chinese and prepared a little sermon on it which I duly delivered the next day. As usual on the following morning, Wednesday, I awoke with a feeling of relief and satisfaction that the ordeal was over for another week.

It was while Auntie Eva and I were sitting at breakfast an hour or so later that we heard sounds like fire crackers going off. We thought they were unusually loud but assumed there must be some very special celebrations being observed. A few minutes later we were conscious of the swish-swish of cloth-soled feet running across the courtyard to our kitchen, and then our cook burst in, looking pale and anxious, to pass on the news he had just received.

'The Japanese have returned. They are attacking the city. They've entered the north gate already!'

So the sound we had heard was not crackers, as we had thought, but firing.

Auntie Eva was marvellous. I don't remember her showing the least trace of alarm. She had been through it before, anyway: and, as there was nothing she could do about it, she did not allow herself to be diverted from her programme. Whether the Japanese were invading the city or not, whether the guerilas were fighting back or sneaking out of the South gate—she would continue to hold her Wednesday Bible class for the women on the compound. She went off to her room to prepare for it.

With me it was different. I'd never been in a city under attack before, except during the First World

War when, as children, my brother and I had watched as a Zeppelin floated over London and dropped a few bombs, mainly on waste land. I had certainly never seen any fighting. With mingled feelings of apprehension and excitement I was standing around wondering what I should do, when something impelled me to hurry across our courtyard, through the guest hall, out into the large front compound with its school rooms, paved walks and tall church building and on to the front entrance. And as I hurried along, the words of the text I had spoken on the day before flooded into my mind like a powerful stream that submerged every other thought. 'The angel of the Lord encampeth round about them that fear Him, and delivereth them.'

The compound was filling up with men, women and children, who came pouring in through the open gates to the security of the Mission campus. Here and there I saw a bundle of bedding being thrown over the walls to be followed by a man or a boy scrambling down after it. By the time I reached the gates, the stream was thinning out; and when I peered along the street, I realised why. The Japanese had entered the city and, at the crossroads about a couple of hundred yards away, were jumping off their armoured cars, their rifles at the ready. Every now and then a shot was fired along the street—a spray of dust revealing where it had landed.

'Close the gates!' said someone urgently but the plucky gatekeeper was reluctant to do so. There were still people lurking in doorways, then slithering along the walls to disappear into the opened gates of the Mission. If the gates were closed they would be left outside and defenceless.

Yet if the gates were left open and Japanese soldiers came along the street, they might easily open fire if they saw a crowd of people congregated in the courtyard. Then the thought occurred to me that if I stood in that opened gateway and the Japanese came, they would see I was a Westerner from a neutral country and pass on.

So I stood there. I must have stood there for several hours and, all the time, my mind was submerged by verses of Scripture about angels: the horses and chariots of fire round about the prophet Elisha. . .; the angel delivering the apostle Peter from prison. . .; the ladder set up by the place where Jacob lay and angels of God ascending and descending on it. . .; the angel of God standing by Paul in the storm at sea. . .; 'Fear not. . .'

I stood there that day without fear, except for one occasion when, the sense of exultation at the presence of celestial beings carrying me away, I stepped out into the road almost defiantly. The Japanese couldn't touch *me*! The sharp sound of a shot, and a puff of dust only a few feet from where I stood sent me promptly back to the shelter of the doorway, and I realised then that there is only a step between faith and presumption. I was taught a spiritual lesson: not to go any further into the conflict than God indicates. Bravado, or even an excess of zeal, can place us in unnecessary range of the enemy's attack. I resumed my position inside the opened doorway, and did not move out again.

I forget most of the people who slipped in behind me to the security of the compound that day but there are a few that remain in my memory. One was an old man with a white goatee beard who emerged from the house opposite and crossed over the road carrying a little ginger kitten. Another was a young woman who walked steadily along the road with a baby in one arm and a big basket, evidently containing essentials for an overnight stay, on the other. And two little schoolboys, their faces white with fear, sidled silently past me. It did not matter who they were or in what condition they came. The door was there, and it was open, and whoever decided to do so could come in. I was reminded of the words of the Lord Jesus: 'I am the door. By me, if any man enter in, he shall be saved. . .'

It is a day that I will always remember, although I did nothing beyond standing at the gate. Japanese soldiers went down other roads but they did not come down our road at all; and at evening time they retreated from the city to re-enter it peacefully the next day for permanent occupation. But the consciousness I had of the presence of angels was so extraordinarily real that although I heard nothi#g and saw nothing, I knew they were there.

But some actually saw them, although I knew nothing of it at the time. It was two or three years later, when Irene Steele and I were working together in another part of the province, that we saw approaching us, one day on a country road, a little family whom we immediately guessed from their appearance were 'flee-the-famine-people'. The man was pushing a laden wheelbarrow with a child on top and his wife was walking beside him carrying a basket. We naturally stopped to enquire where they came from. When they answered, 'Taikang,' my interest was quickened.

'Taikang!' I exclaimed, adding, 'I lived there once.' I saw that the woman's interest had quickened, too, and said, 'I was there when the Japanese attacked the city.'

'You're teacher Dong!' she exclaimed. I nodded, and she continued, 'I heard about you.' Then she added words which somehow did not really surprise me. They merely confirmed what I had always been conscious of when I looked back to the red-letter day. The presence of angels.

'People said they saw Teacher Dong standing at the compound gate,' she said, then added rather solemnly, 'and two men with wings standing beside her.'

12

Dear Edward,

Someone told me the other day that *Madame Guyon* was the recent book choice on a Radio Monte Carlo programme. The news quite cheered me. I'm never really satisfied with what I have written, and that book is no exception; so it was comforting when I heard that it had been well received.

But to return to events in Taikang, once more occupied by the Japanese who had evidently come to stay this time. The city had to settle down to an uneasy acceptance of their presence, for the guerillas had departed and there was no indication that the Nationalists would appear. We had been in a sort of No Man's Land for months.

In those early days of their permanent occupation, the city was half empty for, as soon as the news had got around that the Japanese were entering by the north gate, there had been a hasty evacuation out of the other three gates. Everyone fled to find temporary refuge with relatives living in hamlets and villages in the countryside.

Late one afternoon Auntie Eva and I went for a walk on the city wall. I sensed the atmosphere of fear that hung like a pall over the place. The silence was eerie, for no one was to be seen, and the streets were deserted. From the wall we could see into the courtyards of the houses adjoining it, and the only person we saw during the whole of that walk was an old woman who emerged from a back door to shake out some grain in a basket. Old women were often left behind in times of trouble to look after the premises. Their presence aroused no suspicion and yet staked a claim until the owners returned.

On our large compound, life continued much as usual, except for the occasional visits of Japanese soldiers who strolled in from time to time when off duty. Their arrival sounded a silent alarm throughout the place, especially in the courtyard occupied by the schoolgirls, who disappeared as if by magic, for everyone knew what the Japanese soldiers would demand if they found them. The alarm was sounded in our courtyard, too, but in this case quite openly. Someone would come hurrying through the guest hall, calling urgently, 'Teacher Dong! Teacher Dong!' and I would know what was required. Whatever I was doing I would drop it immediately and with a silent prayer, 'Lord, help me!' would go as quickly as possible to meet the Japanese intruders. Almost invariably they would look at me with surprise, and I soon learned to take the initiative by asking, 'Do you speak English?'

It worked like a charm.

'Spe-eek Ee-english?' they would respond. They had all learned a little English at school, and were delighted at the opportunity to try it out on an English native. They could not speak intelligibly but they could write a few English sentences so, with the combination of their writing, my speaking and sign language, we would contrive to carry on quite a conversation.

However, the best means of communication was through the Gospel posters on the wall of the guest hall. Many of the Chinese and Japanese characters are the same, so I found that pointing to Chinese characters on the posters aided communication; it also gave me the opportunity to explain the Good News. I had come to China to proclaim the Gospel of Jesus Christ, no matter to whom. He had died for these young Japanese soldiers as much as for the Chinese, and I was really very glad to gain their attention for a few minutes, to explain the basic facts of heaven and hell, and that heaven had been opened for any who would accept Jesus as the only way. There was one pictorial poster in particular to which I turned again and again. Known as the Two-Way Poster it depicted a steep mountain path down which a number of little figures were walking with heavy bundles of sin and guilt on their backs, until they reached the edge of a cliff over which they pitched headlong into a lake of fire. That was the pathway to destruction.

But in the middle of the picture was a cross, before which one of the little figures was kneeling while the bundle was rolling off his back. That was not all. From the cross another pathway could be seen, going up the mountain to end in a golden haze of glory, and one or two little figures were seen ascending it, with no bundles on their backs. That was the way to life.

With posters like that to aid me, it was not difficult to get the Gospel across and, on the whole, I had an attentive audience. The young soldiers listened respectfully enough and, almost invariably, when our conversation was finished they walked quietly off the compound without giving any trouble. I only remember one incident in which a Japanese soldier, foiled in his evident intention to find a girl by my insisting on accompanying him wherever he went, suddenly drew his dagger and threatened me with it.

Somehow I knew he wouldn't use it and I simply walked straight on saying in Chinese, 'Huh! I'm not afraid of you!' Rather sheepishly he put his dagger back into its sheath and took himself off. Perhaps I ought to add that although I felt no fear at the time, I did not sleep any too well that night! These experiences have their reactions.

It was during the time that I was in Taikang that the Nationalists opened the dykes of the Yellow River in a vain attempt to stop the Japanese advance. The countryside was flooded over hundreds of miles, hamlets and villages were swept away and many, many people were drowned. All we knew of what was going on was through reports and rumours that came by word of mouth, but we were not left in doubt as to the gravity of the situation for long. I well remember the evening when we were told that the waters had reached the north gate of our own city and were still rising.

How one's imagination can run rife at such times! I alternately pictured myself drowning or floating back to Hwaiyang on a raft! In the event, the waters did not enter the city at all though they surrounded it and were deep enough and widespread enough to cut us off from outside communication for several weeks. In those days, of course, we had no radio to keep us in touch.

It was during this period that a young Japanese soldier did me a good turn. The first time he came into our campus he must have sauntered in without anyone seeing him, for there was no urgent call for 'Teacher Dong!' So I was quite surprised to see a Japanese soldier coming through the guest hall into our private compound unaccompanied by either the gatekeeper or the pastor who always hovered around on such occasions. As I stood on our verandah, having just come out of the door, I could not help smiling, for he looked so very young, peering around rather like a curious, slightly awed schoolboy who is not too sure of himself. When he looked across the courtyard and saw me, he gave a guilty start, then seeing the amused smile on my face, his own relaxed and a wide grin spread over it. So we stood looking at each other, two people of differing sex and age, from different backgrounds and cultures, yet conscious of our common humanity and of a simple, almost child-like, desire to communicate. We crossed over the courtyard to meet and I started with the usual question.

'Do you speak English?' He answered in the usual way, 'Spee-ek Eenglish?' A shake of the head, then 'Spee-ek Eenglish—not good. . .' I don't remember how the conversation developed. Not very far, but with sign language, a few words spoken slowly and a few more written down, we established a friendly relationship. He came back several times, sometimes bringing a friend, to try out his English. On one occasion, remembering what I'd heard about cherry blossom time in Japan, I tried to describe the flower, and suddenly he guessed what I meant.

'Sakara? Sakara?' he exclaimed, then said, 'Tomorrow'. Making a gesture as though handing me something, he reiterated, 'Tomorrow—sakara!' And sure enough he turned up the next day and presented me with a postcard on which was a picture of cherry blossom.

One afternoon he turned up to tell me that he was leaving to go to Kaifeng, the large city some hundreds of miles to the north. He had come to say goodbye.

How was he going to Kaifeng, I enquired, with the countryside flooded so that no vehicles could get through?

An aeroplane was coming for him.

But there was no airfield at Taikang. How could he board a plane if it did not land somewhere?

The plane would fly low, dangling a rope, and he would grasp it and be hauled up into the plane, and off he would go.

This conversation was conducted mainly by sign language and I thought I must have misunderstood what he was telling me. But when I repeated the antics of someone clutching a rope dangling from a plane and being swept up into it, he nodded emphatically. Yes, that was how he would get to Kaifeng.

Then I told him of what was on my mind. I was worried about my parents, away in England. If news reached them of the floods, and they did not hear from me, they would wonder if I was drowned. We wrote to each other every week,

whatever the circumstances, but now there was no
way of getting a letter to them. No mail was getting
through now. The floods had cut communications.

I put my hands over my heart, bowed my head,
and screwed up my face as though weeping, trying
to convey the anxiety of parents bewailing the loss
of their child. He watched me, puzzled, then a look
of understanding flashed over his face.

'Letter!' he said. 'Your letter. I take . . . Kaifeng,'
and he mimed the posting of a letter.

So he took my letter, and I never saw him again.
But he was as good as his word. That letter, with a
Kaifeng postmark, reached my parents in record
time, though many were not getting through in
those difficult days.

I knew that the Japanese perpetrated some horrifying cruelties during the Second World War,
hard to understand and hard to forget, but I was
spared either seeing or experiencing any of them.
My lasting memory of the sturdy warriors from the
land of the rising sun is of a friendly young
Japanese soldier with a wide grin who, in the midst
of the tensions and dangers of war, enjoyed trying
out his English.

However, it is not really of Japanese soldiers that
I should be writing, for the contacts I had with
them were quite incidental as far as I was concerned, and had no significant bearing on my
future. The person who made the deepest impression on me and who, quite unconsciously, launched
me on my career as a writer was a Chinese beggar
woman.

The first time I saw her was at the noon prayer
meeting which Auntie Eva and I attended each day

in the women's guest-hall. The few Christian women who lived on the compound were already gathering when I noticed among them a short, oldish little woman whose face was unfamiliar. Very poorly dressed, with a piece of old blue cloth tied round her head, she had—I was impressed to notice—a strangely peaceful expression on her face. Her eyes looked out from above her large, round cheeks with a calm acceptance of whatever life might bring. It had brought, as I soon learnt, a great deal of sorrow.

'This is Mrs. Peng,' I was told. 'She is one of our out-station Christians but has come to the city now, with her little grandson, to live in the workhouse. She's awfully poor and her home has gone now. She is full of praise to the Lord for making it possible for her to live in the workhouse.'

I saw her hands then. One or two of her fingers were missing, most of them were strangely shortened and practically useless. Years ago she had been poisoned, while working out in the fields. So now, her possessions all sold and the money all gone, she had no option but to leave her poor shack of a home in the country and come to live in the workhouse: a great barn of a place with brick beds covered with straw as the only furniture. But at any rate she had a roof over her head and there would be a bowl of thin porridge twice a day. She could go out begging, passing humbly from court-yard to courtyard with her begging bowl, waiting patiently until someone noticed her and went to get a piece of bread or the last scraping from the cooking pot.

One day she grazed her arm and came along to

the little dispensary to see if I could bandage it up for her. It festered rather badly and often had to be attended to. She never complained and was always so grateful for the little attention given—her round, flat face and childlike, trustful eyes beaming a quiet gratitude as she thanked me for going to so much trouble. One Saturday, however, she came along looking rather a queer colour and, while I bathed her arm, she told me that she was very cold at nights. The weather was getting very chilly at the time. She went on to assure me that it was nothing much, and that when she got up and moved about at nights the cold wasn't so bad.

But the following day, Sunday, she did not arrive for the morning service and nothing was seen of her for several days. During that time we had some warm clothes made for her—the indispensable *kai-tih*, the wadded coverlet in which to wrap up at nights, as well as some wadded trousers and a wadded jacket. The Bible-woman and another Christian woman went to take them to her, and on their return they told me, 'Mrs. Peng has been ill, but she's better now. Praise the Lord!'

'And was she pleased to have the things you took?' I asked. Yes, she was very pleased. She had been so cold at night that she couldn't sleep, but when she couldn't sleep, she prayed.

'Now look, Mrs. Peng,' the Bible-woman had said, unfolding the bundle under her arm and disclosing those wadded garments and the *kai-tih*. 'See what your Heavenly Father has sent to you, in answer to your prayers. He heard your prayers, and He's sent you these.'

Mrs. Peng had been rather surprised at that.

'But I didn't pray for any warm clothes,' she said.

'But you were so cold you couldn't sleep. If you weren't praying for warm clothes, what were you praying for?'

'Oh, I prayed for the two missionary teachers, that God would bless them. And I prayed for the pastor and the pastor's wife and all the brothers and sisters in the church. That's what I prayed for.'

'That's right,' said another old inmate of the workhouse. 'I heard her. She was praying for the two missionary teachers and for the people in the church. She didn't ask for anything for herself.'

Perhaps you can understand what I felt like as I walked back to our warm, comfortable home in our private courtyard. While I was snugly tucked up in bed, fast asleep, that old, sick beggar woman, too cold to sleep, had been asking God not for the alleviation of her own sufferings and not for warm clothes but for His blessing on me. I was shamed in the face of such selflessness—a selflessness to which I knew I had certainly not attained. Mrs. Peng was illiterate, couldn't have read the Bible if she had had one, knew nothing of the finer points of theology and would never have thought of addressing a meeting, though she did not hesitate to urge others to put their trust in the Lord Jesus, in private conversations. She viewed the 'missionary teachers' with great respect, as those who understood the doctrine, preached and taught others, and had left their own homes in a faraway land to come and serve God in China. It wouldn't have occurred to her to consider herself in the same exalted category as they. They were beings on an altogether higher plane! Alas, if only she had known. . .!

But for all my shortcomings, I recognised true spiritual maturity when I saw it and, as I knelt by my bedside that night, I found myself melting into tears of joy as I remembered the words, 'There are many that are first that shall be last—and the last first.' How enthusiastically I would be cheering on the sidelines as Mrs. Peng, the beggar woman, went forward to receive her reward! I could thoroughly understand why such as she would be first and such as I, last.

Not surprisingly, when the time came for me to write my usual quarterly newsletter for distribution among my friends back in England, the only thing that really seemed worth recording was the story of Mrs. Peng and her prayer when she was too cold to sleep.

That letter was to have unexpected results.

13

16 March 1987

Dear Edward,

It was good to see you again last Thursday—thanks for the lunch, especially the chocolate and nut sundae with that mountain of whipped cream to crown it. I'm glad we've decided on a deadline for the completion of this memoir. I'll sign the contract as soon as I receive it from you, and will make its writing a priority.

One thing I'm particularly thankful for is that, almost as an afterthought, I brought up those 'Learn to Read English' lessons for you to see. I wrote them about twenty years ago, inspired to do so by a W.E.C. missionary who said to me, 'There's a world-wide desire to learn English. If you could write a little course for beginners, based on the Gospel narrative, you'd have something that could reach millions.' Well, it hasn't reached millions yet, as far as I know, but it has reached thousands through the post and it has been published in Japan and Vietnam and used over the radio in India. A missionary working among Afghan refugees told me recently that she uses the lessons all the time in her work; I've no idea how many others may be doing the same. I put no restrictions on it: it was my personal contribution to the spread of the Gospel worldwide. I was very thrilled, a year or so ago, when a friend of mine, a teacher, decided to develop the material by producing cassettes with readers to go with it. She'd found the lessons very useful for teaching English to Vietnamese refugees. To my surprise, she has now produced what amounts to a set of teaching materials of over 100 pages, complete with alphabet, word construction, grammar, etc., all based on those twelve lessons. It's because she's run into difficulties about getting the material printed that I asked your advice, and I was surprised and encouraged at the interest you showed and the possibilities you saw in the idea.

'Those little lessons could prove to be the most important thing you've ever written,' someone said, and since they are reaching with the Gospel some who otherwise would never hear it, I think that might be so.

To return to my memories of Taikang. My time there was very significant, but it did not last long. The political situation was changing, with the attitude of the Japanese authorities towards Westerners no longer as impartial as it had been. To make a play on a famous phrase, all Westerners were neutral but some were more neutral than others. War clouds were gathering in Europe. Nazi Germany, with Hitler as its Fuhrer, was emerging as a militant power, annexing first Austria, then Bohemia and Moravia, with Poland under threat. The ill-fated Munich Agreement between Britain and France, Italy and Germany had succeeded in postponing the intervention of Great Britain and her allies, but the German invasion of Poland was the last straw, and in September 1939 the Second World War broke out in Europe. Although Japan was not yet officially involved, there was no doubt that her sympathies lay with Germany. During this time things had been getting more and more difficult for British nationals living in Japanese occupied China.

All this had its effect on us missionaries, and the outcome for Auntie Eva and me was that Mission leaders in Shanghai decided to transfer us to join the three in Hwaiyang, and to put a Swiss member of the Mission in charge in Taikang.

So the evening came when we rumbled along in a cart laden with our luggage along the busy, crowded streets of Hwaiyang, lighted by flaring torches, to come to a halt at the front gates of the China Inland Mission premises there. And among the little group waiting there to greet us was Eastern Light.

'Teacher Dong!' he said, his face beaming. 'You've come back, Teacher Dong?'

My face was beaming, too, as I replied, 'Yes, I've come back!' I did not know until later that, since I'd left, he had not ceased to pray that I would return.

'Are you peaceful, Teacher?' It was the polite, conventional greeting, and I replied in the same vein.

'Peaceful! Are you also peaceful, Eastern Light?'

'Peaceful!' Then he added impulsively, 'I'm so glad you've come back!'

'And I'm so glad to be back!' We smiled at each other, and took up just where we had left off.

But it was only three or four months later that I

had to go away again—and this time not only I, but the Tomkinsons, Auntie Eva and Irene Steele as well. The Japanese, who had occupied the city some months earlier, politely but firmly intimated that we were not welcome. We tried to stay, but they were adamant, and quietly organised an anti-British demonstration against us, with a few of the local riff-raff parading round the Mission premises shouting anti-British slogans while friendly neighbours, to show their sympathy, handed a huge jar of steaming, tasty soup over the back garden wall. There were several days of alternating hopes and disappointments before we finally left. But when soldiers were put on guard in our compound and would enter our rooms to see what we were doing, we knew we would have to go.

On the last Monday we were there Eastern Light arrived carrying a jug of milk. All our friends knew we liked to have milk in our tea, a taste they could not understand but smiled at indulgently. We had disposed of our goats in preparation for our departure, and the church deaconess and her family wanted to ensure that we were not without milk for our tea.

'Only an insignificant thought from my father,' he said politely, as he handed it to us. Then he added, 'My heart is very sorrowful because the teachers have to go.'

'My heart is sorrowful, too,' I told him, and we stood talking together for a while. It was not a conversation without hope, however. At such times there is always a bright star in the dark sky for those who know Him who has said, 'I will come back and take you to be with me that you also may be where I am.'

In the course of our short time together Eastern Light announced that he had held Sunday School in his house the previous day, with his small brothers and sisters as pupils.

'What did you teach them?' I asked. He hung his head on one side, and replied rather shyly, 'I told them to repent of their sins and believe in the Lord Jesus.'

Our departure came suddenly in the end. We had expected to remain two or three days more to wind up affairs and pack what we could get into a trunk apiece. Everything else would have to be left behind, we knew—furniture, books, ornaments, crockery and cutlery, clothes, personal belongings. It was a salutary experience for me and revolutionised my attitude towards things. I've never attached so much importance to things since that time.

By three o'clock on what proved to be our last day in Hwaiyang, we were on mule carts with what baggage we could assemble, rumbling out of the city. Only a few of the Christians had heard we were leaving suddenly and had courageously come to say goodbye. So, as our carts passed slowly through the north gate, we thought we had seen the last of the people we had come to know and to love.

But we were wrong. There in the crowded north suburb we saw a little figure standing on a bank at the busy crossroads, bowing towards us. It was Eastern Light. A few minutes later, as the carts drew in to the inn where the animals were to be fed, the little boy came alongside, and looking up at me said, 'I do praise the Lord! He has guided me.' The consciousness of divine guidance was evidently very real to him as he explained. 'I don't know why, but my heart was feeling very unpeaceful when I was out feeding the goats. I felt I only wanted to go into the city to see how you were. So I went back and told my mother where I was going. Usually I go by the short way across the fields into the city, but today I thought I would go by the main road, and I had just got to the crossroads when I saw your carts. If the Lord had not influenced my heart to leave home when I did and go by the main road, I should have missed you and not have been able to escort you a little way.' The courtesy of accompanying departing visitors is very important in Chinese eyes. 'I did not know at all that you were going today,' he added. He was quite calm and composed, shyly polite as usual, but evidently buoyed up by that sense of having had his heart strangely moved: 'The Lord influenced my heart to leave home when I did, and go by the main road . . .'

At last the animals were fed, and the carts rumbled out on to the road again, Eastern Light walking alongside. Then we made the conventional remark; 'Please don't escort us any farther, Eastern Light.' He walked on a little farther then halted and said, 'I won't escort you any farther, Teacher.'

I looked back to reply, 'No, don't escort us any farther. Please go back. I'll be seeing you.' But of course, I knew I wouldn't. Not in this life.

'I'll be seeing you again,' I called, then added, 'In Heaven!' He stood there, looking after us, smiling still and bowing, and called back, 'In Heaven—I'll see you again.'

I think of him sometimes, even now. I expect by this time he is a grandfather, the head of his family. I've wondered how he fared in the dark, dark days of the cultural revolution or even if he survived them. But when I think of him, it is always as a little Chinese boy standing on a bank, with his head on one side, bowing and calling out, 'In Heaven—I'll see you again!'

14

Dear Edward,

I am a Londoner, born in Hammersmith, a townswoman through and through. I think it's in my blood, derived from my mother for whom the capital had an irresistible attraction. She was the youngest daughter of a Cornish farmer. As a little girl, standing on the banks of the river Fal, she would look towards London and say to herself, 'I'll go there one day . . .' When her father, who was an alcoholic, reduced his family to poverty, she obtained a job in the accounts department of John Lewis in Oxford Street and, apart from two or three very brief visits, never returned to Cornwall. She preferred the city. This apparently unnecessary preamble is not so irrelevant as it may appear, for it helps to explain my reactions, after being turned out from our mission centre in a little city in agricultural Henan, at finding myself in the great, teeming port of Shanghai.

I was delighted! I had not realised how much I enjoyed the freedom of walking around paved streets, travelling on public transport in the shape of tramcars, talking to people in my own native language and, best of all, not being stared at by everyone. No longer was I an object of interest and curiosity as soon as I emerged from the seclusion of our compound to be watched and commented on as I walked along the street, and to draw a little crowd of interested spectators if I stopped to look at the goods on a wayside stall. In cosmopolitan Shanghai of the 1930s, Westerners were a common sight and for us, returning there after several years inland, it was a fascinating and exciting place. Naturally, we did not patronise the famous race course, join the smart clubs, or enter into the merry-go-round social life of the professional and business men or of the armed services stationed there. The large compound of the China Inland Mission—with its two huge buildings providing office and housing for the headquarters staff and accommodation for the steady flow of missionaries en route for the interior or for furlough—was the centre of our lives. But excursions could be made to the shopping areas downtown, to the tree-lined avenues of the French concession or to the restaurant that specialised in old-fashioned English cream teas—if and when we could afford such an extravagance.

To offset these advantages there was the problem of clothes, for in Shanghai no Westerners wore Chinese garments, and up-country missionaries opening the trunks they had left behind found that the clothes they had carefully packed away in tissue paper were now embarrassingly out of date. However, no-one expected missionaries to be smartly dressed, and there was always someone to make helpful suggestions or alterations or to lend an article of clothing so that one could sally forth comparatively confidently on Sundays to attend services in the Cathedral or one of the other English-speaking churches.

There were attractions of a different and more inspiring nature in Shanghai, too, in the shape of the various Christian missions and institutions centred there. For those of us who had been living in an inland city where the small, struggling church to which we were attached was the only outward evidence of Christian activity, it was exhilarating to see and hear about what was going on in the Christian hospitals, schools and colleges as well as in the seamen's and rescue missions of the port. There was so much to interest and encourage, for if things weren't going too well in one area, they would be flourishing in another. And there were the special meetings held on two evenings a week in the large Prayer Hall, at which our own missionaries returning from the interior gave their reports of the work they had been doing. Shanghai, from my point of view, was a good place to be. I was in my element.

There was an even more intimate reason for my happiness in being there. It had to do with a woman named Elizabeth Robertson and what I saw as God's guidance in my life. Elizabeth Robertson was a Scot who had embarked on a rescue work among prostitutes that no-one else was attempting. The Door of Hope Mission had been started some decades earlier, to provide a refuge for Chinese girls who manage to escape from the brothels into which they had been sold, and was by this time well established in Shanghai. But there was a little stream of white women prostitutes, some of them pathetic refugees from the Communist Revolution in Russia, for whom nothing was done—until Elizabeth Robertson started to get in touch with them. I had heard about her while still inland and had been corresponding with her. Now, through no deliberate choice on my part, I was brought into contact with her personally and the work she was doing. I met her first at a prayer meeting at which she announced that she was praying for a fellow worker. She felt the need of a colleague, someone like-minded and with a desire to reach these women with the Gospel of Jesus Christ, someone who would be prepared to go to them where they were, risk the dangers of such encounters, and show them genuine friendship.

So the little group of us prayed about the matter and, as we did so, my spirits soared. Surely I had been brought back to Shanghai for this very purpose! 'Behold, I have set before thee an open door' came readily to my mind and by the time we had risen from our knees I was convinced that I was the one to be the answer to those prayers. I talked it over with Elizabeth and the little group of people who were giving her moral and financial support, and they agreed that if the General Director of the C.I.M. would release me, I should join her.

Obtaining permission from the General Director to move away from Chinese work to which the Mission was committed, was not so easy. He was obviously reluctant to see a young worker, only three years out, getting involved in something that might eventually lead her out of the Mission altogether. However, there was no reason for withholding help for a spiritual enterprise of which he thoroughly approved in principle and as there was no Chinese work into which I could be drafted at short notice in Shanghai, he agreed that until it was reasonably safe to send me back into inland China, I could work with Miss Robertson. And as she was looking for a flat and therefore had no accommodation to offer me at present, I would, of course, remain living in the Mission home.

Things had gone very smoothly so far. There was every evidence that the Lord was opening the door before me and that all I would have to do would be to enter it. Even if it eventually meant leaving the Mission altogether, the transition to another work would be simplified by the fact that my father was supporting me so there'd be no financial problem.

Only one thing was lacking, and that was the indefinable conviction, based on a personal commission from the Lord Himself, that this was the way for me. I wanted to be sure that He was leading me, so I decided to pray for a definite indication. I thought of the words that had come to mind in that prayer meeting—'I have set before thee an open door . . .' If only they would come to me again, not just in my mind, but either before my eyes, or in my ears! So I prayed that I should either see them or hear them during the next week, and having prayed, I started to write in my diary. 'Prayed that if it were God's will I should do this work with Elizabeth Robertson I should either see or hear, before next Saturday evening, the words . . .' But at that point something interrupted me and I did not finish the sentence. However, I knew just what the words were and, all the following week, I was alert to see or hear them. It seemed most likely I should do so. Surely at one of the daily prayer meetings or at the special meetings in the Prayer Hall they would be quoted; or in some book or magazine at which I might happen to look, they would appear!

I was full of expectation. Sunday, Monday and Tuesday passed uneventfully, then Wednesday. By Thursday evening I was beginning to get anxious. Only two more days in which to see or hear those words and know that the step I had taken was the right one. Saturday evening came, with the regular big public meeting in the Prayer Hall. The hymn books we used at these meetings all had a text at the top and, as each hymn was announced, my eye roved eagerly over the whole page, hoping the text would be somewhere there. As each person preached or gave a report I listened for that text. I listened for it as one and another led in prayer. But the words never came; no one even mentioned the book of Revelation in which they are to be found.

When the meeting was over and we dispersed from the Prayer Hall, I avoided the groups chattering together and hurried away. I wanted to be alone. I mounted the wide tiled stairs of the Mission Home to the second floor, walked along the corridor to my bedroom and entered with a sense of dismay in my heart. The time was up. I'd asked the Lord that He would let me either see or hear those words by Saturday evening and I had neither seen nor heard them.

I walked over to my desk, sat down heavily, opened the drawer and pulled out my diary. For some reason I had not written in it all the week—

there had been nothing special to report, I suppose. So when I opened it, I saw the last entry I had made, a week before. It read: 'Prayed that if it were God's will I should do this work with Elizabeth Robertson I should either see or hear, before next Saturday evening, the words . . .'

But the words were not there either. The significance of that blank, unfinished sentence was inescapable. I felt as though I had suddenly come to the edge of a cliff and a great void was before me. God had definitely *not* confirmed the step I had taken. What was I to do?

It was one of those occasions when I could only cry to the Lord to extricate me from the dilemma I had got myself into. I had committed myself to work with Miss Robertson, and the difficulty of my situation was accentuated because she had been taken ill and was in a nursing home, so the task of finding a suitable flat somewhere in Shanghai had fallen on me. I could not withdraw now and leave her in the lurch. I must continue flat hunting, and doing what I could to keep in touch with one of the women she had been trying to help. She had landed herself in jail but could at least be visited once a week by special permission of the authorities. She had a cell to herself but was exposed to the view of anyone passing up and down the corridor, for she was literally behind bars, as though in a cage, like an animal in the zoo. She was surprisingly matter of fact about her situation, and seemed by no means abashed by it.

My memories of those weeks spent in Shanghai are rather hazy. All I can say is that though nothing I did in connection with the White Russian prostitutes prospered, I was mercifully preserved from any disasters. In one case there was an eleventh hour deliverance from what would have been an impossible situation. Miss Robertson, before being taken ill, had undertaken to be responsible for the White Russian prisoner if her sentence could be shortened, fully expecting that by that time a suitable flat would have been found into which to receive her. But now Miss Robertson was laid up in a nursing home, we had no flat, the authorities were planning to hand over the prisoner on a certain day as arranged, and there was no one but myself to receive her and take her—where?

On the night before I was due to go to the prison to collect her, I was at my wits' end. I had not the slightest idea what I would do the next morning. I'd have to go to the prison, of course, as arranged, but what then? Where did I go from there with my charge?

I should like, at this stage, to be able to record that it was my faith in God, my confidence that He would see me through, that enabled me to sleep that night, but alas, I can make no such claim. As far as I remember, having prayed about the situation again, in a confused and desperate way, I seemed incapable of worrying any more. There was nothing else that I could do, and I felt beyond caring about the outcome, so I went to sleep.

If there is one verse in the Bible more than another that comforts me where faith is concerned, it is found in 2 Timothy chapter 2 verse 13, where the Authorised Version reads, '*If we believe not, yet He abideth faithful, He cannot deny himself.*' To me that simply means that however wobbly my faith may be, He won't let me down. Theologians may have a different interpretation to it, but that's mine, and I'm sticking to it.

Certainly it proved correct early the next morning. I was called to the 'phone before breakfast and told that I need not go to the prison after all. Instead, the pastor of a White Russian church in Shanghai would go there with his wife, accept responsibility for the woman and take her to their own home.

I do not know what strings had been pulled in the human realm to bring this about but, from my point of view, it was God who had extricated me from the alarming predicament.

Another incident comes to mind as I write which reveals, alas, the weakness of human nature, and that some, at any rate, of my inner struggles could have been avoided altogether if I had paid more attention to the voice of God in my own heart. This is what happened.

I had been on my knees in my room praying one morning, when I heard the gong for dinner, the midday meal. Now meals in the Mission Home were always served very punctually. The housekeeper, an efficient Scot, was a stickler for time and, although Jeannie Anderson was a warmhearted person who would go to great lengths to help anyone in real need, she could become very irate with those who were late for meals, and even more so with those who did not turn up at all. She knew the exact number to be expected every time, even though there were often over seventy of us, and if one place were vacant, she would notice it. So when I heard the gong that day, I stifled the

very strong conviction that I should remain in my
room, in prayer. I knew that if I failed to appear at
the table, not having signed the book to indicate
that I would be absent, I should be in for a
dressing-down. I hesitated long enough to be in
danger of being late, for I would willingly have
skipped the meal had it not been for fear of Miss
Anderson's stern rebuke. As it was, I decided I
didn't want to face it so hurried downstairs, across
the hall, along to the dining room and slipped
rather breathlessly into the only vacant seat I could
see at one of the long tables. I was only just in time
for grace. When I raised my eyes afterwards, I
found myself sitting next to a young missionary
whom I had not met before.

Like me, he was in his first term of service; like
me, too, he was waiting to be re-designated to an
inland mission centre in an area beyond the
Japanese occupied zone. We were about the same
age, both single, we found each other quite
interesting, and an indefinable attraction that was
very disturbing sparked off. It was all very superficial really, and I think we both knew it, but it was
acute all the same. We saw very little of each other,
for in those days easy friendships between the
sexes were frowned on by those in authority. There
would have been no thought of being alone
together. One or two outings in a party of half-a-
dozen or so were the most that he arranged and
our conversations were limited to casual meetings
in the public rooms of the Mission Home. But the
consciousness of each other's presence was revealed as our eyes met, even when we were chatting
in different groups. And it triggered off something

in me that I had imagined I had safely put aside.

It was the thought of marriage. It was becoming evident that my desire for the work with Miss Robertson in Shanghai itself, with all its excitement, variety and the freedom to move about without being stared at, was not to be fulfilled. Already there was talk of places beyond the Japanese-occupied areas in need of missionary help, and of those of us who had been turned out of our centres being deployed among them. To go back to a remote inland city, and the loneliness of being a single woman there, seemed to me like stepping into my coffin. It wouldn't be so bad if I had the companionship of a husband. And the thought began to insinuate itself into my mind that perhaps that conviction that the Lord intended me for a single life was not to be permanent after all.

But it *was* to be permanent. The day came when I was told plans were being made for me to return with Irene Steele to the province of Henan, to a small city on the Anhwei border, where we would be the only Westerners, of course, and half a day's journey from the nearest mission station where a young married couple were living. And I knew that was the end of my hope of working in Shanghai, and the end of the alternative of going back to the interior with the prospect of marriage, too. It was not a matter of remaining single to do the work in Shanghai or going back to the interior with a husband. It was a matter of relinquishing all hope of that work in Shanghai *and* going back to be a single woman missionary in the interior.

I always look back to that period as being one of the most difficult in my whole life. I was reading, a day or two ago, in the book of Proverbs. Coming to the words, 'The fining pot for silver, and the furnace for gold: but the Lord trieth the hearts,' I thought about that time. The consuming of dross and the refining of gold is a painful business when it comes to the human heart. But during those dark, grey days, as I was preparing to sort out my belongings, decide what I would leave in trunks in Shanghai, what I would need for living inland, the Lord met me through a little booklet given to me by a bed-ridden old lady.

The old lady was the wife of D.E. Hoste, Hudson Taylor's successor as General Director of the China Inland Mission. He had only just retired from his position, and he and his wife were living in a flat over the Mission Home, to which young members of the Mission were invited, one by one, for short visits. One day I was invited to go and see Mrs. Hoste. I found her in bed, a gentle old lady who really knew very little about me. I can't remember anything she said to me in that short interview, but she had on the table beside her a box of tracts and booklets and, as I was leaving, she drew one out and handed it to me. It was only a simply-produced, eight-page booklet containing a compilation of short devotional extracts and poems but, as I read it later alone in my room, one of the extracts seemed to hold a message of comfort for me. It referred to the question sent to Jesus by John the Baptist when he was in prison: 'Art thou He that should come, or do we look for another?' The gist of the message contained in that extract focused not so much on the words Christ sent back as a personal message to John—'Blessed is he, whosoever shall not be offended in me'—but on what Christ said *about* John after the messengers had left.

'What went ye out into the wilderness to see?' he asked the bystanders. 'A prophet? Yea, I say unto you, more than a prophet . . .' and he went on, in glowing terms, to make the assertion, 'Among those born of women there has not risen a greater than John the Baptist . . .'

But John himself never heard these words of praise, did not know what Jesus had said about him in his absence. All he knew was that the One who was giving sight to the blind, healing the leper and raising the dead, had given him no promise of deliverance from imprisonment. He had to be faithful to death, and wait for his reward beyond it. He did not even hear those words of commendation, revealing the approval of the Master.

I was conscious of hearing no words of commendation from Him, either—only the challenge of going forward to obtain the blessing of the unoffended. The thought came that perhaps the Lord was approving even of me, as I set my face to that lonely path back to inland China. There was comfort in that thought.

There was something else in that little booklet, too—words that I have quoted many times since. They helped to explain the experience through which I was passing, and alleviate the sense of desolation.

There is a peace which cometh after sorrow
Of hope surrendered, not of hope fulfilled,
A peace that looketh not upon tomorrow,

But calmly on a tempest that is stilled.

A peace there is, in sacrifice secluded,
A life subdued, from will and passion free,
'Tis not the peace that over Eden brooded,
But that which triumphed in Gethsemane.

And so I said goodbye to the city and the work I had hoped to do, and went back again to the province of Henan.

15

Dear Edward,

Glancing back over the last instalment of my memories of China, I realise it was written in a very minor key. Actually, I finished it in Easter week, just before Good Friday with its reminder of the principle that the seed must die if there is to be fruit. Resurrection is always preceded by death, and dying is a painful process.

Appropriately enough, today is Easter Monday, and I can write now of what happened after those devastating days when I felt as though I were stepping into my coffin as I left Shanghai for the interior of China. Though the weeks that followed were grey ones for me, the time came when I emerged quite suddenly from my cocoon of depression. And it happened in the last place I would have expected—in the Mission compound of Siangcheng—that very remote town near the Anhwei border that had seemed to lead into a featureless wilderness as far as I personally was concerned.

I had had the gloomiest expectations of it. It was a small and unimportant place, off the beaten track, and therefore we could expect nothing in the way of interesting, unexpected visitors. There was a little group of Christians in it, though not enough to have a proper church building, so they met in a converted barn on the compound rented by the Mission. There were four or five outstations connected with it—villages some distances from the city where even smaller groups of Christians met for services on Sunday. It did not sound very inspiring.

Irene Steele and I knew what was expected of us. We were to help illiterate woman who had become Christians with their reading, give them Bible teaching, visit them in their homes, organise Sunday Schools, go to the outstations for the same purpose, and to preach, if appropriate. But we were to be careful not to take any lead in church affairs. The aim of the Mission had been clearly defined at an important conference held some years previously. The aim was that the churches it had brought into being should become self-governing, self-propagating and self-supporting. To this end, financial support from the Mission for Chinese workers was being gradually withdrawn and missionaries were being instructed to relinquish, as soon as possible, the leadership role they had inevitably adopted in the earlier days and to encourage the Chinese to take responsibility for church affairs and for evangelism. Missionaries were to be available for advice when asked for it and to preach when invited to do so but were not to interfere in church matters.

The aim was right, of course, but not very easy to achieve. Some of the missionaries who had remained in the centres in which they had been in control, had a difficult time of it, like Mr. Tomkinson in Hwaiyang and the pastor compromising with idolatry.

However, no such problems were likely to arise in Siangcheng, for Deacon Liong, the chemist, Deacon Hsiao, the seller of cloth, and Deacon Fan, of independent means, were staunch in their Christian faith; and with the redoubtable Elder Dong of the village of Dong to support them and ensure that things were kept on the right lines, there was no idolatry in the church there. Inevitably there were other problems; family and marital as well as personality clashes when people with varying convictions came into conflict about church activities, discipline and the use of church funds. But I cannot remember any serious matter that was not dealt with far better by the church leaders than if it had been left to us missionaries.

So to Siangcheng Irene Steele and I went. We had spent some time in the neighbouring city of Shenkiu, where the young missionary in charge was an American. It was his responsibility to make sure that things were in order for us in Siangcheng and he took this seriously, seeing to it that the premises we were to occupy were habitable, and that a suitable cook was employed. It all took time, but the day came when we cycled the twenty miles, along narrow paths through fields and over bumpy roads, to enter the west gate of the city and push our bikes along the dusty streets till we came to a halt at what looked like just another shop with the shutters up and one door left ajar. We had arrived. The old gatekeeper, who spent most of his time dozing in a deck chair by the door, rose to welcome us, and we passed through the large bare entrance hall into a narrow compound bounded, on one side, by the blank wall of the house next door and, on the other, by two or three rooms used for small meetings. That led to the converted barn with its rows of backless benches, through to a neat little courtyard where Mrs. Han the Biblewoman lived with her schoolgirl daughter, and across to a gate which led to our own courtyard.

It was different from the other Mission compounds in which I had lived, with their paved walks and colonial-style houses, their balconies and verandahs. This was typically Chinese, with two little tile-roofed, three-roomed houses at right angles to each other, and an acacia tree in the middle. Beyond this little courtyard was a field in which to keep the goats which would provide us with our milk. The whole narrow compound, from front to back, was bounded by high walls effectively screening us from our neighbours. There was nothing about the place to make any natural appeal but it was as I entered it that the cloud of depression that had been enveloping me finally dispersed.

A day or two before, while reading in John's Gospel, a little phrase from chapter 14 had struck me with a sense of personal significance: 'I go to prepare a place for you.' I knew it referred to the future life in heaven but, somehow, as I read it, it seemed to hold a promise for the immediate future, too. The words came vividly to mind again as I walked through that narrow compound and felt a sudden upsurge of spiritual vitality; a sense of being in step with my Master such as I had not known for a long time. I was in the right place at last!

I lived in Siangcheng for nearly five years. Irene Steele was the missionary in charge (so she had to do the accounts!) for the first year. Before she left, among other things, she had organised a women's preaching band which became an integral part of church life. When she was designated to another area, I became the senior missionary with Doris Weller as my colleague. Doris and I had been in Language School together but afterwards she had been sent to teach in the school for missionaries' children in Chefoo, north China, so had had no opportunity to study or practise Chinese. Now, after several years in institutional life, she had to start all over again in a backward inland city without the advantage of qualified teachers, and with only one English companion.

Looking back, I realise how very unsatisfactory a fellow-worker I was to both of them, with my regrettable tendency to barge ahead with silent concentration and do my own thing, leaving them to do theirs. It speaks well for them that after all these years they are still my good friends, and we keep in touch with each other.

It was very early in this period in Siangcheng that I received a letter which I think was the most important I ever received in my life. It came from London, from the Editorial Secretary of the China Inland Mission's headquarters there. He had seen a copy of the letter I had written over a year earlier about Mrs. Peng, the beggar-woman who prayed for others when she was too cold to sleep, and it had given him an idea. If I could write eight or ten brief character sketches of some of the other Chinese I had met, he could make them into a little book. It would provide people at home with a glimpse of what God was doing in China and would meet a real need at this time.

That letter came to me not so much as a commission from the Editor as a commission from the Lord Himself. He was telling me to do the very thing that came most naturally to me; to use the particular talent that my parents had recognised when, as a little schoolgirl, I would spend a whole evening concentrating with frowning intensity on the essay that was required as homework for next morning's English class. I don't know whether we work hard at something because we are good at it or whether we are good at something because we work hard at it. Maybe the two go hand in hand. Certainly, the only sort of homework to which I willingly applied myself as a schoolgirl was that which involved writing.

'What is that in thine hand?' the Lord asked Moses. In his case, it was his rod. In my case, it was my pen. Now the Lord was telling me to take it up and use it as He directed and I responded with complete freedom and happiness. I felt as though waters that had been dammed up had suddenly been released to start flowing; or as though I had emerged from a tunnel out into the sunlight. A stream of satisfying activity was opened up that day that has continued right up to the present time.

I am actually sitting in an Underground train, *en route* to meet a friend, scribbling this, but that marvellous mechanism of memory is conveying me back fifty years, and I am again in the little whitewashed dining-room with the door opening on to the small inner courtyard of the Mission centre in Siangcheng. My typewriter is on the table before me, the sun is shining, and my heart is singing as I write about a tranquil-faced old Bible-woman emerging with unselfconscious dignity from the church compound to 'preach the Way' to her neighbours; about a grubbily-dressed vegetable-grower who has won many people for Christ through a gift for healing which the Lord has given him; about the village inn-keeper who can't often get to church, but has taken down the Old Heavenly Grandfather idol from the place of honour in his guest room and put up a Gospel poster in its place; about the Christians in the village of Fan who insisted on entertaining a snow-bound party of missionaries for several days, brushing aside apologies for the inconvenience caused with the simple words, 'You are for the Lord. We also are for the Lord.'

Altogether, there were ten little character sketches in that—my first—book, which was published in 1940 under the title *They Seek a City*. It is long since out of print, of course, but I have a copy; and as I turn its pages I see them again, those lovable Chinese Christians, my friend Eastern Light among them, and I am so thankful that I can say of them all—'I'll see you again—in Heaven!'

And that is how I started writing books—launched on my career by a Chinese beggar-woman.

16

Dear Edward,

I've just been re-reading one of the books I wrote, years ago, about my time in Siangcheng. The book was mainly concerned with people not events; and as I have browsed through its pages, they have come to life again—those Chinese men and women with whom my life was interwoven so intimately in the quiet backwater of a remote city in China during the years when the Second World War was raging.

Not that we were without our dangers and alarms, for Siangcheng was in even more of a No-Man's-Land than Taikang had been. The nearest garrison of the Chinese Nationalists was in Shenkiu, some twenty miles away, while at about the same distance in the opposite direction the Japanese had their outposts from which, every now and then, they would make a foray towards Siangcheng. We had no telephone or radio, of course, but news travels quickly by word of mouth, and signs of activity on the streets, as the well-to-do and able-bodied moved rapidly with cart and wheelbarrow out of the city to disappear in the countryside, were sufficient to alert us to the necessity of packing a few essentials, locking up our rooms and departing on our bicycles for Shenkiu where we would wait until things settled down again.

However, this did not happen often; most of the time we were only affected indirectly by the Second World War. Funds were low and the post was uncertain, though I must pay my tribute to the International Postal Union, at any rate as I saw it operating in those unsettled days in China. In times of danger the local Post Office, along with all the other official departments, would disappear into the countryside and continue operating from some remote village until it was safe to return to the city again. Although many letters were lost, the marvel to me was how many got through. My parents and I wrote to each other once or twice a week, whatever the circumstances, and we were rarely more than two or three weeks without receiving a letter. Often I would get two at a time, one from my father, who went to a lot of trouble to find out the best route by which to send it, giving clear instructions that it was to go 'via Siberia and Mukden' or something of the sort, and one from my mother, simply marked 'Via quickest route'. They usually arrived by the same post.

On the whole, therefore, life was quiet and undisturbed in Siangcheng and, being largely isolated from the outside world, we had plenty of opportunity to get to know our Chinese fellow-believers. They had only been names to us before our arrival in Siangcheng, and there were few enough of them, but as the weeks passed those names became distinctive personalities.

Deacon Liong, the chemist, was tall, slim, dignified, looking out on life with an impersonal gaze.
Whatever happened, Deacon Liong never lost his
self-possession and unconscious air of superiority.
Even when standing at the door of the Gospel Hall
preaching to the passers-by, which he did from
time to time (he was surprisingly open in his
Christian witness), he somehow managed to convey
the impression that he was doing them a favour.
He spoke little in committee but was the dominat-
ing figure in the church and, in any matters of
policy or administration, it was he who ultimately
got his own way. A rather awe-inspiring person, he
lacked the warm geniality of the good mixer and
was feared rather than loved. But he was stalwart
in his faith in the invisible but living God and
resolutely opposed to anything savouring of
idolatry. True, his morals had gone awry at one
stage, when he'd taken another wife and stopped
attending church, but he'd repented and done
what he could to put things right. It had been a
hard road for him, for his second wife, a coarse,
rather slatternly-looking woman made things as
difficult as possible, waylaying him in the street and
airing her grievances in a loud voice for all to hear.
This was a terrible loss of face for the proud,
naturally secretive man, but there was nothing he
could do except endure it, which he did with an
impassive face. The genuineness of his repentance
was revealed in his changed attitude towards his
delicate, long-suffering little wife. He was very
solicitious of her health, showing her a care and a
courtesy most unusual for a husband in old China,
writing to her frequently when he was away from

home because, as she explained rather coyly on one occasion, 'he knows I get worried'.

Deacon Hsaio, the seller of cloth, was entirely different. No one was afraid of him, not even his wife, though at one time she had dreaded his return from a business trip—wondering whether he would be in a good mood, or whether she would be in for a beating. But that had been before the Christian convention. He had attended this, expecting to have a good time—only to discover himself to be a wolf in sheep's clothing and to learn that true religion, like charity, must begin at home. He had been quite different after that. Of a sanguine, easily influenced temperament, he had remained remarkably steadfast in his Christian faith and conduct when others, who were naturally quieter and steadier, had fluctuated and fallen. The church in Siangcheng had had its ups and downs and, at one period, when things had been at a very low ebb, he had been one of the very few who had remained loyal and had patiently borne jibing over his adherence to 'the foreigner', the missionary in charge.

He was a very practical man, and we could always turn to him for help in getting things done, although he was not so quick to respond to invitations to preach at the Sunday services. He did not consider preaching to be his line. He preferred to exhort people in private, and many were the illiterate old women who came regularly to worship on Sundays because he had first exhorted, then prayed for them. The more educated church-goers might find him rather tedious, but the common people heard him gladly as he harangued them with the homely illustrations they so readily understood. He was what we would call a personal worker, and rather prided himself on his understanding of human nature, and ability to handle men and affairs tactfully. One could discern a certain patient, conciliatory expression creep over his face when this was happening, along with a kindly smile. I was often conscious of being tactfully handled myself and of allowances being made for the evident fact that I had what was called a quick temperament, not a placid one.

I don't know how I would have managed during those years in Siangcheng, without Deacon Hsaio.

Deacon Fan was different from either of the other two. He was a man with a longish, rather melancholy face, who rarely had anything to say except on the few occasions when he got excited and said too much. His life seemed bound up in the church and he was always on hand to tidy up or sweep the chapel; but when it came to the deacons' meetings he would sit silently with his head down, eyes on the ground, and take no part in the discussions. If he was asked directly for an opinion he would say, 'I follow,' from which it was concluded that he agreed with the majority. On one occasion it was pointed out to him, with slightly amused asperity, that he couldn't follow two points of view, so in this case, who or what was he following?

'I follow the Lord,' he'd replied. This pious pronouncement, while failing to help towards a decision, proved unanswerable.

We wondered how he would manage when, according to the current system of local government, he was elected as head man over ten families. He was known to all his neighbours as a man of integrity, which is why he was elected. In fact, he did not like the office because, as everyone told me with a shake of the head, he couldn't fulfil it without telling lies and practising deception. In the circumstances, such conduct was generally recognised as being quite legitimate. The important thing was to keep everyone as happy as possible and ensure that nobody lost face. But the more Mr. Fan progressed in the Christian faith, the more unhappy he became at the lies he had to tell. His civic duties interfered with his church activities, too. So when we heard, after a time, that he was no longer headman, we felt relieved on his account.

But he was still not happy. The reason emerged one evening at the 'lamplight service', when about a dozen of us gathered round a table to read from our opened Bibles with the light from an oil lamp.

'I have sinned,' he said simply, and there was a sudden breathless hush. What had he done? Those who suspected the worst were quite relieved as he continued, 'I have got out of the position of headman, but I told lies to get out of it, and I know that was sin.'

Immediately a comforting murmur arose from those whose eyes were fixed on him, and someone said reassuringly, 'That's not sin. You had to tell lies to get out of the position and you had to get out of the position because you had to tell lies while you were in it!'

Mr. Fan was not convinced. He looked across at me, the only missionary present, and the only one who had remained silent.

'What does Teacher Dong say?' he asked. I could feel my forehead screwing up in a perplexed frown. I felt for him, wanted to comfort him, but I knew I must be faithful. It's no use glossing things over, pretending things are all right when we know they are wrong.

'We ought not to tell lies,' I said slowly and reluctantly.

'But if he didn't tell lies he'd never get out of the position,' volunteered someone. So what was there to do? The lies had been told, there was no way back, and poor Mr. Fan, burdened with a sense of guilt, still stood looking silently at me. I knew of only one way for him.

'The Bible tells us in 1 John, chapter 1 that if we confess our sins, God who is faithful and just will forgive us our sins, and cleanse us from all unrighteousness,' I said. So that is what we did together—claiming the promise. I never heard the matter referred to again. The forgiveness of God towards the penitent sinner is inherent in the Good News which we go to proclaim.

Many efforts were made to induce Mr. Fan to lead Sunday services but they all failed. On a few occasions he was persuaded to lead the prayer meeting that preceded it but, as this usually consisted of announcing a couple of hymns, reading a passage of Scripture and then inviting others to pray, it did not call for any powers of oratory. Surprisingly, however, he was always ready to take his stand at open air meetings, leading the singing, inviting passers-by to come and listen to the doctrine, handing out tracts—all without any trace of the embarrassment he felt when occasionally standing on the platform in church. On one memorable occasion, when there was an unexpected breakdown in the preaching, he surprised and delighted us all by stepping into the breach and speaking for about twenty minutes in a most convincing manner, presenting his arguments as though they had been well thought out and prepared beforehand. Such an excellent beginning promised well for the future; but Mr. Fan retired once more into his shell, declared that he could not do it again and refused to have his name put down on the list of speakers.

Deacon Liong, Deacon Hsaio, Deacon Fan—they are not the only ones who have come to life again as I've read through that little book I wrote nearly fifty years ago. But I'll have to leave out most of the others to make room for Mrs. Han, the Bible-woman. She was our nearest neighbour, whom we saw every day and who became my closest fellow-worker.

I met her first at Shenkiu, where she had come on a visit shortly after the funeral of her husband, whom she had nursed through a long illness. I remember—at a prayer meeting—being surprised, almost shocked, at her cheerful, composed manner and at the fact that she thanked God for relieving her of her heavy burden. It seemed to me that even if she were glad to be rid of an ailing husband, it would have been more seemly to keep quiet about it! However, I learned later that she had been devoted to him, and that what she'd referred to had not been the lifting of the burden of service, but the lifting of the burden of grieving widowhood. She had discovered the reality of the verse in Isaiah that speaks of the One who bears our griefs and carries our sorrows. The crushing weight of sorrow had been lifted and she could face life standing upright.

Her husband had been employed as gate-keeper evangelist on the mission compound in Siangcheng and, as it was arranged that she should remain there as before and that her old father-in-law could 'watch the gate', no great change in her life was necessary. Like Phoebe of old, she was the servant of the church. A capable and diligent woman, she willingly undertook the mundane tasks of the church compound, putting aside her own affairs without hesitation to welcome guests who arrived unexpectedly, heating water for them to wash their faces, pouring tea, producing the wadded quilts which she kept well mended and clean so that they might sleep in comfort. On Sunday mornings her sitting room was filled with chattering women who came to see her before the service started. Often enough one or two of the poor or lonely ones came back afterwards at her invitation to help her prepare the midday meal—and, of course, remain on to help her and her schoolgirl daughter to eat it. Her good deeds were performed with such graciousness that they never seemed like merit-gaining charity.

She was a cheerful person, not given to reflective thought or introspection, and her faith was of such childlike quality that I sometimes felt it was almost immature. This was especially so in the case of her encouragement to the women in prison to pray that God would get them out. She and I used to go every Monday morning to visit them, complete with Gospel posters for me to preach from and tracts for those who could read. On the face of it, the women's prison was not too bad a place. It looked just like the inner courtyard of any Chinese home, and the prisoners were free to wander in and out of the rooms and talk to each other or sit out in the sunshine mending clothes or spinning cotton, while the elderly wardress, looking just like one of them, mixed with them in quite a friendly way. Altogether, the atmosphere was quite different from the dark prison in Shanghai where, although living conditions were less primitive, the prisoners were isolated from each other behind bars, and cut off from the fresh air, the sun, and the singing of birds.

So much for the outward appearance of things. There was one thing the women had not got that they all longed for—freedom. After I had preached, Mrs. Han chatted with them, and it soon became evident that there was just one thing they wanted God to do for them: 'If we pray to Him, will He get us out of this place?'

'Yes,' said Mrs. Han firmly. 'You pray to our Heavenly Father, and He will get you out of this place.'

I felt very uneasy about this. It seemed to me to be too tall an order to expect God to release them, since, after all, they were in prison because they had broken some law or other. One woman, we were told, was a murderess. I tried to explain the necessity for all of us to repent and to put our faith in Jesus Christ who had died on the cross for our sins; to assure them that the real result of doing this would not necessarily be early release from prison but peace of heart; to stress that we must be prepared to place ourselves in God's hands, and trust Him to do what is best for us, though it might not be just what we would choose for ourselves; and that the important thing was to be sure of our eternal destination . . . and so on. On the way home I broached the subject again, and Mrs. Han agreed with everything I said. But the next time we went to the prison and the women told her they were praying that God would get them out of that place, she by-passed all the theology I had tried to instil and assured them that God was able to get them all out of that place and that He would do so if they really prayed to Him.

And He did. The whole lot of them.

This is what happened. There was another rumour that the Japanese were going to raid Siangcheng again. There was the usual evacuation from the city of the able-bodied and well-to-do. We two missionaries got on our bicycles and went to Shenkiu, where we remained until news came that the Japanese, having entered Siangcheng, and stayed there for thirty-six hours, had retreated, so it was safe for us to return.

On the Monday morning after we were settled in again I went through the gate from our compound into Mrs. Han's, and said, 'We'd better go and visit the workhouse and prison again, hadn't we?' To which she replied that it wouldn't be any use going to the prison, as there was no-one there.

'No-one there! But there were about sixteen of them. There must be some of them there.'

'No, Teacher, there's no-one there. You see, it's like this. When the prison authorities knew the Japanese were coming, they all wanted to get away as quickly as possible, but they couldn't take the prisoners with them and they couldn't leave them behind either. So they just released them all, and told them to go home. There are none of them left in that place now. They've all gone.'

I was silent for a moment, letting the news sink in. Then I said slowly, 'So God answered their prayers. He got them out of that place . . .'

'Yes,' said Mrs. Han with a calm smile. 'God answered their prayers.'

As I walked slowly back through the gate into our compound, I wondered if the real reason behind the short and apparently purposeless invasion of the Japanese into Siangcheng on that occasion was simply that God had heard the cry and answered the prayers of a group of heathen women who believed what Mrs. Han told them about Him.

It was not the only time when prayer was answered in a dramatic and utterly unexpected way during my time in Siangcheng. On one occasion the answer came in a violent storm. I'll tell you how it came about.

We had a neighbour who was a good friend to us. Dr. Wang was a well educated woman from Manchuria, and a qualified doctor, who seemed to feel a special responsibility for us two missionaries and would hurry round to see us if she heard we were ill and make sure that we had money in hand when she suspected funds were low. She did not come to church very regularly. Perhaps the contrast between our informal meetings in the rough-and-ready atmosphere of the barn, and the dignified church services to which she had been accustomed brought home to her too acutely the change in her circumstances since fleeing from her home in the north. But there was no doubt about her faith in Jesus Christ, and her allegiance to Him. Although she did not consider herself a teacher, and made no attempt to preach to her patients, she politely suggested they should go along to the Gospel Hall and hear the Christian doctrine, since, she assured them, 'It's good to believe in Jesus.'

One day she came through to our compound, pulled aside the bamboo screen which we hung in front of the door to keep out the flies, and greeted me rather urgently. Waving aside the customary invitation to sit and drink tea, she said, 'I haven't come on a social visit, Teacher Dong. I've come because we must pray. There is plague in the city.'

'Plague!'

'Yes. It has only just started, and I don't want to spread the news and cause a panic. But I've seen two patients already, and I recognised that it was plague. They died within hours. We can't do anything to stop it spreading, and if it does spread hundreds of people will die'. Then she added deliberately, 'Only God can stop it.' That was why she had come: to pray. So we knelt together in the little guest room, and prayed that God would stop the plague. Then she rose to her feet, explained that she must go off immediately to see a patient and, in quite a matter of fact way, took her departure.

Two or three nights later, I was awakened by the sounds of rushing wind and a pitiless downpour of rain, followed by the crashing of tree branches and the crumbling of masonry. Our rooms were built strongly enough to resist the storm and I had no cause for personal alarm but, as I lay in bed and listened, I knew I was hearing the whipping off of thatched roofs and the collapse of buildings made with mud bricks. It was the worst storm I had ever experienced, and I remember thinking, 'Oh, these poor people! First, the plague, and now their homes being flooded!' I wondered what news would be brought in from the street to Mrs. Han the next morning, but nothing disastrous seemed to have occurred to anyone we knew. And, rather to my surprise, as the days went by there was no mention of plague.

Then one day, as I was in the street, going to visit someone, I saw Dr. Wang. She was being wheeled along on a wheelbarrow—the usual method of conveyance in our part of China. She was on her way to see a patient in the country but when she saw me she politely alighted to greet me.

'Dr. Wang!' I exclaimed. 'I've been wanting to see you.' I remembered the urgency of our last meeting and asked eagerly, 'What has happened about the plague? Is it spreading?'

'Oh, that's all over,' she replied. 'That storm blew it away.'

'The storm blew it away?' I must have looked as incredulous as I felt, for I was really taken aback. Dr. Wang was no superstitious peasant, yet here she was talking about a storm blowing away the plague! 'How could a storm blow it away?' Then she went into an explanation about rat fleas, and the breeding places of germs, and the wind and rain blowing them away. Not understanding, I just said 'Oh!' and left it at that. But there were no more cases of plague in the city. Years later, when I told the story to a missionary doctor, he confirmed the explanation that Dr. Wang had given.

'Yes, it's scientifically correct,' he said. 'The germs would be carried by rat fleas, but a fierce storm like the one you describe would disperse their breeding places, and that would be the end of it.'

None of the people of Siangcheng knew what that storm had saved them from. Very few even knew that those two or three people who had died so suddenly had been struck by plague. I've sometimes thought that perhaps the sudden storms which sweep over our lives are breaking up secret breeding places of evil which we scarcely realise exist, and saving us from far greater disasters.

17

19 May 1987

Dear Edward,

I mentioned in an earlier letter that before she left Siangcheng Irene Steele formed a Women's Preaching Band; and as one of the most memorable incidents in my time in China occurred when I was out with them, I'd better introduce the members of the band now. Here they are:

Mrs. Hsiao, Deacon Hsiao's wife—happy-go-lucky, rather unreliable, but very lovable, sympathetic and human. I had a specially soft spot in my heart for her, even though she was apt to fluctuate spiritually: sometimes being whole-hearted and keen; at other times, slack and indifferent. She was more gifted than any of the other women: quick to grasp a point, intelligent, and with an indefinable quality that made people confide in her. She was a most valuable member of the Preaching Band, for she spoke clearly and with an unexpected conviction which solemnised her listeners to an unusual degree. And her easy-going disposition enabled her to get on with the other members of the Band—even Li *Tai-tai*, who was socially a cut above the other women, having been the wife of an important official, which is why she was a *Tai-tai*.

157

Li *Tai-tai*, to be frank, was one of the church's problems. Not that there was anything wrong in her manner of life, for she had long since left behind all questionable practices. She neither smoked nor gambled, was honest in her dealings, had separated from idolatrous superstitions, and was a comparatively strict Sabbatarian. But she was touchy. Mrs. Han and Mrs. Hsaio, who tried to cover up for her, apologetically explained that she had what they termed 'a little bit of a temperament'. They spoke about it as though it were a snappy little dog that lived with her—sometimes safely asleep but liable to wake up at any time and bite whoever happened to be around.

'Li *Tai-tai* has a little bit of a temperament' they would say, 'She doesn't mean anything.' And usually she didn't mean anything, as the people in the Street of the Oilhouse, where she lived, had come to find out.

'Her heart's all right,' they agreed after she had gone to a lot of trouble to help one and another who was ill or in distress. And as she was a lover of law and order, heartily supporting any efforts that were made to correct the rather haphazard form of worship and procedure that prevailed in the church, the deacons viewed her with respect. Her powers of endurance were remarkable. Often, when out with the Preaching Band, she would suffer from a racking cough that kept her awake for hours but she never allowed it to prevent her from putting in a full day of preaching, walking from village to village sometimes in bitterly cold weather.

The third regular member of the Band was the

diminutive Widow Wang. She had lost her husband very early in life but by dint of thrift and hard work had managed to provide her only son with sufficient education for him to earn his living as a clerk in a store rather than a farm labourer. She had taught herself to read, too, and was quick to help any other woman or girl to do so. (Teaching illiterate women to read their catechisms and New Testaments was recognised as being of primary importance to the church at Siangcheng.) When out with the Preaching Band, she could always be relied on to chat to inquisitive people who wandered round to see what was going on, besides doing most of the practical work of carrying water, lighting the fire, preparing and cooking the food. However, when it came to the actual preaching, she was distinctly unconvincing, for in the middle of her exhortations she was liable to break into a self-conscious giggle as she realised she was the centre of interest then take fright and disappear as fast as her sturdy little legs would carry her.

Although from time to time others were invited to join the Band, these were the three permanent members, appointed by the elders and deacons to go with the missionary once or twice a year to one of the outstations, and preach in the nearby villages. We usually divided up two and two, with one of the outstation Christians to accompany us, and off we would go, armed with a roll of pictorial posters and a handful of tracts, on our evangelistic forays.

On the whole, we met with quite a friendly reception. People might be indifferent to our message but they found us entertaining, especially me: the first Western woman most of them had ever seen. It would take some time to satisfy their curiosity as to how old I was, what food I ate, my marital status and how much I had paid for the cloth of my gown; but when the questions had all been answered, my companions would explain that I had come to exhort them to follow The Way, which was the signal for me to unroll the pictorial poster (The Two Way Poster was the one I used most often) and start to preach.

I remember standing on a little hillock with a group of peasants silently looking and listening as I pointed to the figures in the picture who were going down, down the mountainside to the edge of a cliff, from which they fell into a lake of fire.

'A picture of mortal life, with death at the end of it', I explained, and then went on to proclaim the news I had come to give.

'But the True God did not want people to perish like that. He wanted to save them. So He sent His only Son into the world. Think of it! The True God had one Son, and He sent Him into this world to save us. He was born as a baby, like us, and He was given a name—Jesus. Jesus was like us in everything except that He never did anything wrong. He grew up, and did good to people: He made blind people see, deaf people hear, sick people well. He only did good. He healed many people but He did not want money for healing them. He healed them because He loved them.

'But His enemies hated Him. They wanted to kill Him. They made a cross of wood. Then they took nails, and nailed His hands to the cross.' As I held out my hands, first one and then the other, I saw some of the women wince, then screw up their faces at the thought of the pain caused by those nails being driven in; and I realised they were hearing of the crucifixion for the first time.

We have heard it so often that we have become inured to it, alas, but the physical sufferings of Christ really touched those Chinese country women; and when I spoke of His death, then His burial, there was a sorrowful hush. Death and burial—they had seen it so often, those old women with their lined, patient faces. They knew the emptiness, the hopeless end of those they had known and loved. I paused for a moment, for I seemed to savour it with them, but then a feeling of exultation rose in me.

'But that wasn't the end!' I cried. 'After three days He rose again. He came out of the tomb. He was alive!' I saw the amazement on their faces and continued, 'And He is alive today. He went up into Heaven and He's there now. You can't see Him but He can see you. You can't hear Him but He can hear you. If you pray to Him, He will hear you. If you believe in Him, He will forgive your sins, and take you to be with Him in Heaven.'

Well, that gives you an idea of how we set about condensing into an unannounced fifteen minute talk the basic facts of the Gospel for those who had never heard it before—and might never hear it again. Visits to homes would follow, when there would be fleeting opportunities to enlarge on the message we had come to deliver, then on to the next village. When we got back to our base, there would be a meeting after the evening meal for people living on the spot. Then at last, when all the stragglers had departed, we could spread out our bedding, take off our outer garments, and thankfully lie down and fall asleep.

On the occasion of which I write, we had got to that point after a very tiring day. Our base was the little mud-brick Gospel hall itself, which had been built in a field not far from the village, so it was all very quiet and peaceful. I had sunk into that deep, delicious sleep that follows extreme weariness when the sound of knocking on the door, and a man's voice demanding matches reached down to my consciousness.

Matches? It was midnight, the door was shut, we were in a field, not even in the village: who would be waking people up to ask for matches at such a time and in such a place?

'Have you got any matches in there?' the voice demanded, reiterating the question. By this time I was sufficiently awake to be very annoyed at having been disturbed. I shouted, 'Go away!'

'Have you got any matches in there?'

'Yes we have, but we're not giving any to you! Go away!'

'I want some matches! Open the door!'

Open the door and let someone in to get some matches? At midnight! Not likely!

'What sort of a person are you, coming at midnight to a place where there are only women, asking for matches?' I retorted indignantly. 'No, we won't open the door. Go away!'

'If you don't open the door, I'll throw it in,' said the man. And he did just that. The roughly made wooden doors fitted into sockets, and it required only a strong hand and arm to lift them out. There was a clatter and a thud, and the double-leaved door lay on the ground to reveal a tall man with a gun in one hand and a powerful torch in the other.

'Where's that man?' he demanded, shining his torch round until the light came to me, glowering at him over my quilt. He had thought it must be a man, talking to him like that. And I still went on talking: 'What sort of behaviour is this? No decent person would come in the middle of the night to a place where women were sleeping!'

By this time he was walking round the room, pocketing any oddments he noticed lying around— torches, hand towels, cash. Having made the round, he walked out.

'Oh good, he's gone,' I said. 'Can you put that door back in its sockets?' I knew the women were accustomed to that type of door. 'Then we can go back to sleep.' It was the one thing for which I craved. Sleep! Then I saw that my companions, unlike me, were all up and fully dressed. Even as I spoke, Mrs. Hsaio slipped across the room and hissed, 'Teacher! Teacher! Get up! Get up! He's coming back, and there are others outside!'

Reluctantly I slipped out from under my wadded quilt and reached for my outer gown, still so sustained by my irritation that I had no fear. Besides, I had remembered something.

The angels at Taikang!

If I had had no need to fear the well-trained, ruthless Japanese soldiers, why should I be afraid of a mere Chinese bandit? I felt quite defiant and, when he returned and started going round the room again, picking things up, I was all ready to start arguing with him again. Then, quite suddenly, God spoke to me.

And He spoke to me in Chinese.

I don't mean that I heard a voice, for I didn't. But as I stood by my camp bed, buttoning my gown and glaring indignantly at the man, my mind was suddenly and powerfully flooded with a sentence from the Sermon on the Mount. The words were in Chinese, but I understood them, for I had read them many times in my Chinese Bible.

'Do not resist an evil person.' They came with such overwhelming authority that I knew without the shadow of a doubt that God was speaking to me, and that I had no option but to obey. With a very bad grace I did so, standing in sulky silence as the man swept my money off the table into his pocket, looked round to see if there was anything else worth taking, and departed.

We departed, too, after being sure the bandits had really gone, and spent the rest of the night in the security of the village, lying in a row on a heap of straw in a barn. It was all very ignominious, quite the reverse of the quiet triumph of the experience in Taikang. It taught me that God does not always deal with us in the same way.

Not very long afterwards it was brought home to me how near I had been to death that night. A young Swedish woman and her two-year-old child, passing through Siangcheng, came to our compound for a brief rest. While eating the meal we hastily provided, she told us her story. She had been travelling with her husband in an area not so very far away and at midnight bandits had come to the inn where they were staying. The young husband had gone to confront them and, without hesitation, they had shot him dead.

I realised then that but for that sudden authoritative command—'Do not resist an evil person'—the same thing could have happened to me.

18

Dear Edward,

As a fellow missionary once sagely reminded me, life is a pilgrimage—inward as well as outward. Especially inward. When I look back over those years in Siangcheng, there are two or three brief inner experiences that stand out vividly, while the days, weeks, even months of outward activity have faded from the memory. However, it was the days, weeks, months of outward activity that brought me to one of the spiritual crises of which I will write now.

I was jaded, dull, bored. Indeed, it was worse than boredom; it was fast becoming a depression from which I saw no way out. I felt hemmed in— there in the narrow compound with the ceaseless round of little meetings, of visits to women in small courtyards, of hours spent trying to teach some of them to read, and the lack of any mental or emotional stimulation.

If I had been back in England it would have been different. I could have refreshed myself by going for a walk, visiting a friend for a chat, listening to some music or reading a new book, perhaps, or even spending a few days by the sea or in the hills.

166

But in Siangcheng there were no such outlets. Where could I go for a walk in the narrow streets or even along the paths through the wheatfields, without meeting people who stared at me or expected me to stop and talk and answer the inevitable question, 'Where are you going, Teacher?'

In any case, where was there to walk to? Once outside the walls of the city, the flat wheatfields spread for as far as the eye could see, without even a little hill to relieve the monotony of the landscape. In times of peace, missionaries on the plain had gone for a yearly holiday to a hill station in the south of the province but the war had made that impossible. The hill station was beyond the Japanese lines and inaccessible.

One way and another, I felt as flat as the landscape. We had very few books (we had had to leave our small libraries behind when we left Hwaiyang), and no music. The narrow streets and the dark houses were devoid of beauty and there were no gardens. The only flowers we saw were those that Irene—and later Doris—managed to grow in our small back compound, and our only contact with the outside world was through the few letters that reached us. We have no idea how much these things contribute to our enjoyment of life until we are deprived of them. There was a vacuum in my mind when I was weary, and there seemed no way to fill it. There were times when my memory took me back to what years ago had been the place of my chief enjoyment—the dance hall. The shaded lights, the orchestra striking up, the couples gliding together on to the polished surface of the floor, the music, the gaiety of the foxtrot or the sensuous languor of the waltz . . . I pulled myself up from lapsing into a desire for that atmosphere of merriment and light-heartedness and turned sternly to the duties of the day.

But I was inwardly dry. I maintained my habits of Bible reading and prayer morning and evening, alone and also with Doris, but I needed something more. I felt parched.

One day the barrenness of my own soul became intolerable. I knew I could not go on like this and, having half an hour to spare, I went to my bedroom, threw myself on my knees, and cried desperately, 'Lord! Lord Jesus! You said, "If any man thirst, let him come unto Me and drink." Lord, I'm taking You at Your word. I'm thirsty! And I've come! I'm parched and I want to drink.'

I waited expectantly, but nothing happened, so I cried again, with the same lack of result. I knew that only as I remained deliberately and consciously in the Lord's presence could I expect the answer I longed for, but to remain there silent, trying to concentrate on God, was beyond me. My mind would wander, I knew. I must find a way to occupy it, and decided to pray for other people. Perhaps that was what I ought to be doing, anyway. I had a list of names and addresses of friends at home, so I got it out and went down the list, praying one by one for them, for about half an hour. Then I rose from my knees, went out into the courtyard and got on with whatever it was I had to do. There was no time now to think of myself. Other matters claimed my attention; and it was not until two or three hours later that it dawned on me that I wasn't feeling bored or depressed any more.

Nothing noticeable had happened, there had been no upsurge of joy, but the dryness was gone. I was just quietly contented, back to normal, satisfied to be in the place where God had put me, doing what I believed He wanted me to do. It was as though, silently and imperceptibly, the waters had risen and the stream was flowing again.

That experience marked a new phase in my life, and illuminated for me a sentence which I came across at about the same time in the book of Job. As usual, I was reading in the Authorised Version, and in verse ten of the last chapter I saw the words, 'And the Lord turned the captivity of Job, when he prayed for his friends . . .'

I wasn't focusing on the tribulations of Job, or the resentment he might have felt towards the friends who had misjudged him; a resentment imprisoning his mind. My circumstances were quite different; none of my friends appeared to be misjudging me. But I knew what it was to have a mind in captivity to an unsatisfied desire, to the boredom of monotony, to discontent with my lot. And I knew I had been released from that captivity after I had spent time with the Lord, praying for my friends.

From that time on, I knew what to do when I found dryness and depression beginning to enfold me. Praying for others always had a liberating effect on me. It was the method I employed because I had found it worked. But it merely illustrates what those who believe have discovered for themselves down through the centuries: that 'a little talk with Jesus makes it right, all right.'

The negro slaves who sang, 'Steal away, steal

away, steal away to Jesus,' had reached the heart of the matter, too. And I remember an old Chinese woman living in the Siangcheng workhouse, to whom we had spoken of the Heavenly Lord who opens His arms and says 'Come', telling me rather shyly one day how she had done that.

'I felt I wanted to pray,' she said. 'So when everyone else was out in the courtyard, I went into the room alone and sat down and said, "I've come." But I don't know how to pray, and I didn't know what to say, so I said, "I've come because I want to have a little chat with you." That was all—I didn't know what else to say. But then—my heart became so peaceful.'

'My heart became so peaceful.' That's just how it was with me.

That verse about the captivity of Job always carries me back to that narrow compound in Siangcheng; so, even more poignantly, does a verse in the book of Jeremiah. It came to me one terrible night, after Mrs. Yen had been tortured by guerillas and faced the prospect of more to come if she did not give her youngest daughter to one of their officers as his second wife. And it had all come about because she had acted on my advice. But as that is rather a long story, I will leave it until I write my next letter.

19

Dear Edward,

The appellation 'terrorist' is frequently heard these days. Kidnappings, people being held as hostages, prisoners being tortured—these horrors appear time and time again in the media, reminding us of the perilous days in which civilisation finds itself. The story I am going to relate for you now is one of terrorism. Mrs. Yen was the victim but I, too, was involved, for if she had not acted on my advice she would have avoided it all, as I realised on that terrible night after she had been tortured.

Mrs. Yen was married to a baker and lived in the north suburb of Siangcheng, sharing a courtyard with one or two other little households whom she bossed as firmly and benevolently as she did her own family. She had been a church member for quite twenty years, and was referred to on odd occasions as 'deaconess'—a title which always embarrassed her, for neither she nor anyone else seemed to know how she got it. For years she had been in possession of a catechism which she always brought to church rolled up in a blue towel kept specially for that purpose; but—not being academically minded—she had never learnt to read it and tended to shy off when I offered to teach her. She made it clear that she wished I wouldn't harp on the value of reading the Bible for oneself, which obviously wasn't possible unless one had learnt to read, and tended to avoid me. Had it not been for the little matter of the four dollars, I doubt whether the gulf between us would have been bridged. It was just this little matter that first brought us together.

I learned about the four dollars quite accidentally after a Sunday morning service, when I found Mrs. Yen preparing the noodles she had bought to give a meal to the poor. Four dollars' worth of noodles, she told me and, knowing her own circumstances, I was touched at her generosity.

'That's very good of you, Mrs. Yen,' I ejaculated.

'Oh, I didn't want the money,' said Mrs. Yen. 'What would I want with the four dollars? I said to myself, "I'll give them to the Lord, then it'll be all right." That's why I bought the noodles to give to those poor people. I said to myself, "I don't want those four dollars."'

'What four dollars?' I asked mystified.

Then it all came out. With many embellishments and observations she told me the story of what had occurred a few days before, and this is the gist of it.

Her husband had gone off to deliver orders for steamed breads, her son was in the city hawking fried dough-strings, and she was sitting, as usual, under the awning of rush mats outside the open door of the house—a basket of bread and a cardboard box containing a few coppers and grubby ten cent notes beside her. It was a hot afternoon,

there were no customers and she had dropped off
to sleep. When she woke up and looked at the cardboard box, there she saw a roll of dollar bills. Four
of them! All along with the other change. They
seemed to have dropped from heaven, right into
her box. Her daughter-in-law had been reminding
her that they were nearly out of oil and that Hsiang
needed a new jacket. And now, there were those
four dollars! Mrs. Yen looked up and down the
road, saw no-one, tucked the notes inside her
jacket and sat back, fanning herself.

Shortly afterwards she was conscious of a stir in
the distance. A man was hurrying along, obviously
disturbed, and when he saw her he stopped and
asked, 'Mrs. Yen, have you seen four dollars? I've
lost four dollars. I had them with me when I came
along here about half an hour ago, but I've got a bit
of trouble just now, and I must have put them
down somewhere without thinking. When I got
home the four dollars were gone.'

Mrs. Yen frowned at him.

'How should I know what you've done with your
four dollars?' she asked crossly. 'I've been asleep
and can't remember a thing. I didn't even see you
pass. How should I know what you've done with
your four dollars?' He nodded and off he went.

Off went Mrs. Yen's peace of mind, too.

'I couldn't help the four dollars getting into my
box, could I?' she said, looking at me anxiously.
'I've never stolen anything since I repented and
believed in the Lord. Everybody knows that. And
as for Mr. Li, he's a stupid man. How am I to know
whether the four dollars are his, anyway? If I can't
keep what's in my own money box . . .'

With many involved explanations she told the story: the thoughtless acceptance of what was not hers; the sudden temptation to retain it; then the arguments of self-justification that failed to bring peace of mind.

'So I decided to give the money to the Lord,' she concluded, looking at me rather like a child waiting for the reassurance that that would make everything all right. I felt so sorry for her.

'But Mrs. Yen,' I said reluctantly. 'The Lord doesn't want that sort of money.'

She showed no surprise or even disappointment, but said lugubriously, 'I was afraid He didn't. But what am I to do?'

'It seems to me the only thing to do is to give the money back to the person it belongs to.'

'But what shall I say? It's such a loss of face!' I knew that, and wondered how I would have acted in similar circumstances. But I had no suggestion to make but the obvious one: 'I don't see what you can do but just tell him the truth.'

So that, more or less, is what she did, and it all worked out very well, for Mr. Li was so pleased to see his money again that he congratulated her on her honesty and said she was a credit to the doctrines preached at the Gospel Hall.

That little incident formed a bond between Mrs. Yen and me and although, wisely, she did not consult me on practical matters, it was a different thing when it came to moral or spiritual issues. So when her neighbour's granddaughter was in danger of being taken by a guerilla officer to become his second wife, and she saw a way of saving her, Mrs. Yen came to ask my advice.

'Pao Chen is the same age as my Dzan,' she told me. 'She's always lived in our courtyard with her grandmother, and she's like a daughter to me. But she's got a father, and he keeps an inn in the country, and it was while Pao Chen was staying with him that this guerilla officer saw her. He's taken a fancy to her. He's got a wife already—they both smoke opium.' She lowered her voice and continued, 'They're a bad lot of men, these guerillas.' I knew that a large contingent of them had come into our part of Henan. Ostensibly they were fighting for their country, harassing the enemy, but in reality they were skirmishing about in the No-Man's-Land between the Chinese Nationalist's garrisons and the Japanese, extorting money from wealthy landlords, holding people for ransom, abducting village girls. Everyone was in fear of them. Mrs. Yen knew it but she continued, 'I've nearly got Pao Chen engaged to a young man who lives near us.' Mrs Yen was an experienced middle-man in matrimonial matters. She said, 'If it goes through I could save her. But this officer, Captain Fong ... My family's afraid of what he would do, and told me to keep out of it. If the guerillas get up against me ... What ought I to do, Teacher?'

My reaction was prompt and decisive: 'Don't touch it, Mrs. Yen. You don't want to get up against the guerillas! Keep out!' The words were in my mind, ready to spring to my lips, but they were never uttered, for something happened. I don't know how to describe it except that I suddenly became aware of being silenced by a power greater than my own as the thought of Pao Chen, whom I had never even seen, came to my mind. This un-known girl was not only in danger of being forced into a life of grief and shame but also into a life that would ruin her morally. To leave her in the hands of that opium-smoking guerilla officer was equiva-lent to handing her, body and soul, to destruction. Here in this little room her fate, as it were, was to be decided.

'What shall I do, Teacher?' Mrs. Yen was asking. And I knew that one day I would have to give account to God for the answer I gave to this woman.

'Mrs. Yen,' I said, leaning forward. 'You've got to save that girl.'

So that is what she tried to do. Mrs. Yen suc-ceeded in completing the arrangements for Pao Chen to be betrothed to the young man, then helped to smuggle her, with her grandmother and the young man as escort, away from the city. The young man's parents took fright after that, and fled, too, but Mrs. Yen could not flee. How could she leave her home, her husband, her son and his family and her unmarried daughter to their fate in order to save herself?

The net was tightening. The guerillas, confident of their strength, moved into the city, making their headquarters in a large courtyard right opposite the police station. No-one dared oppose them. There were rumours of what was happening to a lad they had kidnapped, whose ransom had not been paid: 'His leg's broken . . . they're a bad lot of men.' The whispers went round, then silence fell. I did not really know much of what was going on, so when, one day, a frightened white-faced girl came hurrying on to the compound and told me the guerillas had arrested Mrs. Yen, tied her hands together and marched her up to their headquarters, I was furious.

How dared they treat poor, honest old Mrs. Yen as though she were a criminal, and imprison her in a courtyard that was not even the acknowledged place for dealing with civic offences! Where was the justice in such an act? In a white heat of righteous indignation, and without stopping to think what I would do when I got there, I stalked along the street and down to the guerilla headquarters with Mrs. Han (courageous woman) by my side. We were admitted by the soldier on duty without a word. As a Westerner and the national of an allied nation I had 'face'—and I daresay that on this occasion I looked as though I was prepared to use it. We were directed into the very room where Mrs. Yen was standing, hands tied behind her back. A young soldier was lounging against the wall.

He looked thoroughly scared when I demanded to know how he *dared* treat this old lady in such a fashion. He wasn't in charge of the affair, he told us. Kong *Tai-tai*,* wife of the senior officer, was in charge. Still carried along on the wave of my indignation, I demanded to see Kong *Tai-tai*. She turned out to be a girl in her early twenties, sitting beside a charcoal fire in a bowl in the middle of a large room with a couple of beds in it. She rose with a polite smile when she saw me.

'You've come, Teacher?' she said. 'Please sit

*A respectful title for a married lady.

down.' Stools were brought for Mrs. Han and me to join her by the fire and, as we exchanged the usual polite preliminaries of conversation, my indignation oozed away, and I realised that there was nothing at all that I could do. I had no authority and no power. As I sat there, waiting for an opportunity to plead Mrs. Yen's case, all I could do was to pray silently, as I knew Mrs. Han was doing too. I won't go into details as to what turns the conversation took except to say that when I said, 'Kong *Tai-tai*, have *you* got a mother?' quite suddenly her attitude changed. She was silent for a few seconds, then told one of the soldiers standing in attendance to go and unloose Mrs. Yen and bring her in to sit with us. And when I asked that Mrs. Yen be allowed to come back with me to spend the night in the Gospel Hall, she agreed, on condition that she returned next morning.

Next day Captain Fong arrived—a tall, dark-eyed ruthless-looking man. Mrs. Yen was sent for and Mrs. Han and I went with her. I listened for a long time as he and Kong *Tai-tai* discussed Mrs. Yen's affairs, making a show of trying to find out just where the culprit's fault lay and explaining that as a foreigner I really did not understand Chinese customs. Captain Fong said that Mrs. Yen had interfered in other people's business and had forced the engagement of Pao Chen against her father's wishes and that now the girl had disappeared and she was responsible. She must find the girl and return her to her father. If she failed to do that, she would be punished. What punishment she would suffer was not specified and no one enquired.

The atmosphere was sinister. There was a young man in the room whom I had seen the night before and whom Mrs. Yen evidently knew. He was sitting on the edge of one of the big beds, apparently quite free to come and go, but two or three soldiers were between him and the door, and his eyes had the sharp, wild look of a trapped animal. Every now and then he surreptitiously rubbed his wrists. I did not grasp the significance of what I saw then—it was only later I learned from Mrs. Yen that he had been kidnapped the previous evening, strung up by his wrists, and only lowered on the promise of a large sum of money.

It was not so easy to get permission for Mrs. Yen to spend the night again at the Gospel Hall. Captain Fong was evidently unwilling to let her go and it was not until Kong *Tai-tai* had gone and spoken to him hurriedly in a low tone that he gave a grudging consent. But Mrs. Yen must not leave the Gospel Hall and must return as soon as she was sent for next morning. The next morning, she was sent for early; Mrs. Han and I went with her but we were not allowed to remain.

Captain Fong was quite polite to me. He said he was afraid he was delaying me from my affairs at home. When I said no, I was in no hurry, he observed that he himself was rather busy that day. I'd been in China long enough to realise that etiquette was being stretched but I still sat on, with an absent-minded expression on my face. Then I remembered that my sole purpose in coming to China had been to warn men everywhere to repent and believe the Gospel, and that my responsibility to this guerilla officer was not the less because the occasion did not seem very propitious for making known the truths of God's judgment and also His mercy. To do Captain Fong credit, he listened with more interest and courtesy than might have been expected. Yes, he said, he had heard some of this before. What I said was quite right. Then, after a brief silence, he spoke again, very politely and very distinctly, 'Teacher, please go now. I want to interrogate Mrs. Yen.'

I did not fully realise the significance of the word 'interrogate' then; even if I had, I doubt whether I would have acted any differently. I was afraid that if I ignored again that deliberate, repeated request to leave, I should lose what little influence I had. What if I were ordered off the compound and refused re-admission, leaving Mrs. Yen without even the prospect of the little help I could give?

'All right, I'll go,' I said, rising to my feet. 'I'll be back this afternoon Mrs. Yen.' So Mrs. Han and I withdrew, and desperately I sought for a way to deliver Mrs. Yen. Should I go to the *Yamen*?[1] Useless, I was told. The *Hsien-chang*[2] there couldn't do a thing to control the guerilas. The police? Why, they knew pretty well everything that was going on—they were right opposite—but they dared not stir a finger. Eventually I went to see Deacon Liong, thinking he might have some advice for me. We sat in the dark little room at the back of his shop, and in his impassive way he outlined the situation.

'There is one thing you could do,' he said. 'You

1. Chinese mandarin's official residence.
2. Head official in the *Yamen*.

could go to the officer in the Nationalist garrison in Shenkiu, and because you have 'face', as a Westerner, he would have to do something. The guerillas would have to obey him, and Mrs. Yen would be freed.' He paused for a minute, then went on to present the other side of the picture.

'But when it was all over, in a few months' time, the guerillas would come back and take their revenge on Mrs. Yen . . .' We looked at each other silently for a few moments, then I rose to leave. There was no need to say any more. The thought of those reprisals was sufficient. There was nothing I could do.

'We will pray for Mrs. Yen,' he said quietly as we parted, and I knew he would do so.

When I got back to our compound I was told that a man had arrived with the news that Mrs. Yen was being tortured, but if I would pay the sum of 200 dollars it would be stopped. There was no question in my mind as to what my reply should be. I knew that if missionaries started paying out ransom money for church members, there was no knowing who would be kidnapped next or what it would lead to.

'No,' I said firmly. But the thought of Mrs. Yen being tortured was unendurable, so Mrs. Han and I again went to the guerilla headquarters.

Amazingly we were admitted, and taken to the very room where Mrs. Yen was sitting limply on a chair. One look at her told us she had been beaten, for her face had bruises, her cheekbone was grazed and her eyes were dark with pain. In a few brief sentences she told us what happened. The interrogation had not lasted long. Where was Pao

Chen? She did not know. The girl had gone off with her grandmother, she did not know where.

Then she must find her! How could she find her? She would not know where to begin.

Then Captain Fong had ordered that her wrists should be tied together, the rope thrown over a beam in the ceiling, then pulled.

So there she had hung, her toes dangling half an inch from the ground, while they beat her around the head. And under the anguish of that torture, she had said she would give her own daughter, Dzan, in marriage to the Captain instead of Pao Chen.

I went and sat beside her feeling numbed, unable to speak, as she went on talking in short, disconnected sentences.

'But I can't give her . . .

'I'll never give her . . .'

She spoke dully, her eyes dark and burning.

'I thought to myself, why was I suffering like this? It was for those three people. They've got away free. I'm suffering to save them.' She paused for a moment, then went on. 'And I thought of Jesus. I'm suffering for those three people, but He suffered for the whole world.'

Mrs. Han and I sat without moving. It was as though the shadow of a cross had stolen slowly across us as, behind the swollen, bruised face of that Chinese peasant woman, we saw Another Face. Many times we had read the records of the crucifixion but never before had we had so practical a demonstration of what it cost Him to save us as when we saw a dim reflection of His agony in the eyes of Mrs. Yen.

I'm finding it difficult to write this letter, trying to condense into a few lines an experience which it took me seven chapters to cover in a book I wrote about Mrs. Yen nearly forty years ago, called *Beaten Gold*. I have it on my lap before me now, reminding me of things I had forgotten as we sat with her that day in the guerilla headquarters—things such as the arrival of an elderly countrywoman who had walked forty *li**** to see her daughter.

'She works for Kong *Tai-tai*,' she told us, adding in a lowered voice, 'They took her away by force.' But the girl herself looked cheerful enough in her smart bright blue jacket, laughing and talking to a soldier lounging against the door. Whatever may have been her first reactions, she seemed well satisfied with her life now.

'They're wicked people,' her mother continued in an even lower whisper. 'White powder . . .'

White powder. So there was drug smuggling, too, as well as ransom money?

'. . . and brothels,' in a murmur from Mrs. Yen, whose sharp ears had missed little.

There came the falling of darkness; the lighting of flickering oil lamps; the comings and goings of soldiers; a couple of men with provisions dangling from the ends of their carrying poles; then Mrs. Yen's sudden statement, 'Life and death are in this night.'

I remember the atmosphere of fear; ropes hanging down from beams; soldiers out to extort some money on their own account—business more easily accomplished after dark.

*A third of a mile.

My prayer was quiet and urgent; that this night, too, Kong *Tai-tai* would allow Mrs. Yen to come back with me. A soldier remarked that Kong *Tai-tai* was out at a feast, would be very late returning, as she was staying on to play mah-jong. I sat on stolidly, indicating that I was prepared to wait, no matter how long.

Eventually, Kong *Tai-tai* returned. She was surprised to see me there. First, she politely refused to allow Mrs. Yen to return with me; then with a sudden change of mind, she gave the permission, adding, 'But she must come back early in the morning. Captain Fong is going to take her with him to the country.'

So that was what he planned to do. Mrs. Yen had said he could marry her daughter Dzan and he evidently intended ensuring that she did not get out of it. Once out of the city Mrs. Yen would be entirely at his mercy with no-one to interfere, and unless the binding engagement contracts were duly signed. . . . torture!

That was the situation that faced us as we walked back through the dark streets. And that is why, sitting shivering in bed, unable to pray, I opened my Bible where the bookmark was placed at Jeremiah chapter 33 and started to read: 'Moreover, the word of the Lord came unto Jeremiah the second time, while he was yet shut up in the court of the prison, saying, Thus saith the Lord, the maker thereof, the Lord that formed it, to establish it; the Lord is His name . . .'

It seemed so far removed from our present extremity. I felt like turning to another portion, but read on doggedly, and my eyes fell on the words, 'Call unto Me, and I will answer thee, and show thee great and mighty things, which thou knowest not.'

I stared at them and, as I did so, they seemed to penetrate my numbness. I sat up in bed, still shivering slightly. With my open Bible on my knees, I closed my eyes and clasped my hands tightly together.

'O God,' I said aloud, slowly and deliberately. 'O God, here it is in Thy word. Thou hast said "Call unto Me and I will answer thee, and show thee great and mighty things, which thou knowest not." And now, Lord, I'm doing it. I'm calling unto Thee.' Then, raising my voice, I cried as though determined that He should hear. 'Oh God, save Mrs. Yen, in Christ's Name. Amen.'

I closed the Bible, blew out the light, and lay wide awake until the morning. There was nothing more that I could do. God had said, 'Call,' and I had done it.

20

Dear Edward,

I finished the previous letter last night, and as the tempo of this story changes at the point I left off, it seems very suitable to start on a fresh note this morning. And that fresh note must be the observation that God often works so quietly and unobtrusively that we fail to recognise His ways at all. The dramatic, the sudden, the violent impress us but not His skilful working in what appears to be the normal course of events. He seems to work in context, with complete understanding of local customs and conditions. Looking back on the events of the day following my desperate response to those words 'Call upon Me, and I will answer thee,' I find myself smiling with amusement at the way all our problems were eventually solved in a thoroughly Chinese-y manner.

The day started with the arrival of someone to escort Mrs. Yen back to the guerilla headquarters. A short time later Mrs. Han came along with two little parcels of sweet cakes carefully wrapped up in red paper. To my amazement she informed me that Captain Fong had sent them to me with his compliments.

'What's he giving me these for?' I asked her, bewildered. Cakes and compliments! I suspected there was a catch in it, but Mrs. Han assured me quite calmly it was just Captain Fong's expression of good will.

'What am I supposed to do now?' All I needed to do was write 'many thanks' on one of my cards in acknowledgment and give it to the servant to hand to him, she said. Conscious once more that I had completely failed to understand the subtleties of the oriental mind, I did so, thereby demonstrating that we had parted on friendly terms and had nothing to fear from each other.

Meanwhile Captain Fong was treating Mrs. Yen quite politely, as became a future son-in-law and, instead of making her walk, had ordered a wheelbarrow for her. He was taking her into the country, about forty *li* out of the city, he said. He was in good spirits, and strode on ahead, out of the West gate, little knowing that the word of authority had already been spoken in heaven, and that he was walking to his own confusion. How was he to know, with the whole vast plain before him, that when he took the path to the south-west it would lead to the very place in which his prisoner had been born and brought up?* And when he stopped at the inn and ordered rooms for the night, in the village of Hwang, little did he know that word was rapidly spreading among the Hwangs of what was happening to one of their members, to whom about half the population was related in some form or other;

*I can't vouch for the accuracy of the whereabouts of this place.

that already one of them was walking towards the home of a Hwang who was an official of some importance in the Nationalist government and who happened to be back in his native village on a brief visit.

The Hwangs, like most other families, were composed of a few wealthy and influential people and a lot of poor and unimportant relations. Mrs. Yen, of course, belonged to the latter category and, beyond receiving certain advantages in the matter of gleaning at harvest time, could expect little benefit from being related to the Hwangs of higher rank. But the situation she was in now put things in a different light. She was a Hwang and so was the official of some importance. However remote the relationship, family loyalty demanded that he should intervene on her behalf. And as his position with the Nationalists gave him 'face' which a guerilla officer was bound to respect, he was in a position to do so.

So he intervened.

I heard about it from Mrs. Yen herself when, quite unexpectedly, she turned up a couple of days later. It was Sunday, and I found her sitting in her usual place on one of the benches in the church-cum-barn, having arrived early for the service.

'Mrs. Yen!' I gasped. I could scarcely believe what I saw and behaved in a most un-Chinesey manner—rushing up to hug her, half sobbing, 'You're back! You're safe!'

'Don't, Teacher,' she said, somewhat embarrassed, and when I asked her what had happened, she told me quite unemotionally. The influential Hwang had come to the inn to visit Captain Fong who, of course, had welcomed him politely. They had sat together, chatting, sipping tea and nibbling peanuts, and the influential Hwang in the course of conversation had mentioned the matter of Mrs. Yen.

'This old great-aunt of mine who is with you, my wife would like to see her,' he had said. 'She wants her to stay for a day or two. It is too much trouble for you to have her here.' And although Captain Fong had assured him that it was no trouble at all, the word of the influential Hwang had prevailed, and when he'd sauntered away Mrs. Yen had trudged stolidly behind him, to spend the night in the security of his home. Her deliverance from further torture at the hands of Captain Fong had come about just as simply as that. But if the influential Hwang had not happened to be in the district at that time, or if Captain Fong had gone to any other area on the great plain but the one he unwittingly chose, how different it would all have been!

Not that it was the end of the affair, of course. Mrs. Yen still had to be released from her promise to give Dzan as a second wife to Captain Fong and to ensure that no reprisals would follow later on. How that was brought about, I have no idea. Undoubtedly middle-men were recruited to engage in delicate discussions, suggestions and arguments; and probably some money changed hands. It took some weeks to bring the matter to a satisfactory conclusion. But eventually a feast was given at which the influential Hwang and Captain Fong were the guests of honour, and for which all that was required of Mrs. Yen was that she should foot the bill. She was very thankful that it had been quietly agreed that wine should be provided, not 'white powder', which was so much more expensive. The feast made it evident that the whole matter was over and that Mrs. Yen need fear no reprisals. It nearly ruined her financially, but when it was all over she invested in a large print New Testament which she could not afford. She was determined to make good this time. She would learn to read, and she would read the Word of God, the God who had so remarkably delivered her out of her distresses.

The story had quite a happy ending, too, for after some months the guerillas left the neighbourhood altogether, and Pao Chen, the girl for whom Mrs. Yen had suffered so much, returned, well and happy, with her grandmother, her husband and a new-born baby. But by that time the famine was on us. And that is another story.

21

Dear Edward,

I have seen many harrowing pictures of famine-stricken people on the television in recent years, and somehow they seemed quite different from those in the famine we lived through in Henan, China, in the early 1940s. Hundreds of thousands of people must have died in it. Henan is thickly populated, and the famine was severe, made all the worse, of course, by the cutting off of supplies due to the war. Yet it came on us so imperceptibly that Doris and I were unaware of it at first.

It started with a poor harvest. With our English background, it did not occur to us, or at any rate to me, that a bad harvest would seriously affect anyone but the farmers. Prices might rise a bit, but that would be all that the rest of us would know about it. So we thought. The price of grain was as general a topic of conversation in Henan as was the weather in England, so we were accustomed to hearing remarks about its having gone up a cent or come down a cent. But as I walked through the markets that autumn I began to realise that people were talking about it in a different way. It was not only the price that they referred to, but the shortage.

'We haven't got enough grain,' they murmured. Then, more anxiously, 'We haven't got enough grain till the next harvest.' And as time went on; 'We shall starve . . .,' and finally; 'We shall die . . .'

And they did die. Quietly, in their homes.

But before that began to happen I had noticed a change in the streets. Everybody walked more slowly and the bearers of burdens were disappearing. There were fewer men with heavy loads swinging from their carrying poles, or being pushed on wheelbarrows. They had not the strength for the tasks and, in any case, fewer people could afford to employ them. Eventually there were none to be seen except the water carriers. Everyone needed water, so money must be kept for them.

Then there were the beggars. Beggars were a common enough sight in the China of those days and, unlike the pitiable, often repulsive looking beggars of India, they were almost an accepted part of the community, dressed like everyone else, though naturally shabbier. The insignia of their profession was an earthenware food bowl to receive any pieces of bread or scrapings from cooking pots that came their way, and a stick to beat off the dogs. Most households had a dog trained to bark at and even attack unannounced visitors unless called back by their owners. So beggars had to be on their guard. Not everyone was prepared to 'do good deeds' by giving them something, thereby gaining merit, and when beggars were not tolerated, the dogs were not called back. But as the famine increased, there was a subtle change in the beggar community. Parents with insufficient food to feed their children sent them out to hang around the courtyards of wealthier neighbours or distant relations. They wouldn't openly beg for themselves and there were limits to the extent they could trade on family or neighbourly relationships in 'borrowing' what they were likely never to return. But for the children it was different. A hungry child at the kitchen door when a meal was being prepared was not likely to be ignored.

'They'll give a little to a small child,' the parents said hopefully. 'If only the children can get enough . . .'

So it went on. The beggars, some of whom had come earlier from districts that were hit by famine before ours, became too weak to walk around. They crept out of the shacks where they slept, to lie here and there by the side of the road, moaning to the passers-by for just one thing: 'Bread! Bread!'

It was during this period that I read in one of the few newspapers to get through to us of such bumper harvests in North America that mountains of wheat had been burned for economic reasons. That news item made a deep impression on me, and still does when I think of it. Wheat to burn in some places, thousands dying for want of it in others. It challenges me as I think of the plentiful supply of all my material needs in the comfortable position in which I find myself in my old age. It challenges me as I look at the row of Bibles on my shelf, several different translations, and remember that there are fellow believers in places like China who have not so much as a portion of the Word of God in their possession. And it challenges me as I remember that there are millions in the world today who have never even heard the Gospel of Jesus Christ.

I am reminded that to whom much has been given much will be required, and I wonder how I shall measure up in the day of reckoning . . .

But to return to the famine, as it affected us in Siangcheng. Doris and I were already learning to live with inflation. As soon as our remittances arrived we would lay in stores of basic necessities like fuel, grain, oil, salt, rather than keep cash in hand, for money was losing its value all the time. Our remittances came quarterly, and we never knew how much they would be, with exchange rates fluctuating and the war affecting Mission finances. Luxuries like coffee and sugar were ruled out, of course, but we always had sufficient for our needs, which we soon learned were not as great as we had once thought them to be. But there was not much left over and there was little enough we could do to help others.

However—there was something. Unexpectedly a small allocation of famine relief money was granted to us, and we discussed its use very earnestly with the deacons.

Should it be used for Christians only? No: it was decided that as the money had been given to help the most needy, irrespective of their faith, it wouldn't be right to give preferential treatment to our own people.

Should it be used to help a few people effectively or many superficially?

'Most people will have ways of getting a little food, but for some of them it won't be enough. If we can help them eke out what they can get, we may help more people to stay alive,' the deacons said. The daily distribution of a little food would be the best way to do it. Deacon Liong, who studied these things, said there was more concentrated nourishment in an egg than anything else, but it was argued that a bowl of thick, hot porridge would be more satisfying. The idea of handing out a daily egg to the needy was abandoned in favour of a bowl of hot porridge per person per day, to be ladled out to those who came for it early each morning.

It may sound strange to you, but those months in the famine were among the most satisfying of my whole life. I have tried to analyse the reasons, and I think they can be summed up in the one word 'fellowship'. Primarily there was the sense of fellowship with God. I knew I was where He intended me to be, living among the poor just as His Son had done, and I wouldn't have exchanged places with a princess, for the quiet joy that consciousness gave me. Secondly there was the fellowship with the Christians in Siangcheng, as we lived through the famine together. And there was the satisfaction of being able to do something practical, little as it was, to alleviate suffering. That daily allocation of porridge to the hungry did as much for me, though in a different way, as it did for those who received it.

We had a routine to which we stuck rigidly. Early every day the few of us who lived on the compound met for Bible reading and prayer together. This period lasted about an hour, during which one of the women slipped out and got the fire going and the water boiling in the great cooking pot, ready for the carefully measured supply of flour and millet and salt to be stirred in. Then Mrs. Han stood by the pot, ladling a scoopful into each bowl held out to her. Gratefully the recipients sucked in cold air with the hot porridge, licking the bowl when all had been consumed, departing rather reluctantly—some of them to spend the rest of the day begging.

One incident during this period stands out in my memory so distinctly that I can visualise it even now. A prayer meeting was in process. We were gathered in one of the little side rooms between the guest hall at the front and the compounds at the back. There were only a few of us, and as someone was praying aloud I heard the familiar cry of a beggar: 'Bread! Bread!' Looking through the glassless window frame, I saw a boy of about twelve years old walking past, and it was his cry that arrested me. It was different from the hopeless moan of the beggars in the streets. This boy was walking with purpose, and the desperate yet imperative note in his voice moved me to action. Hurriedly I slipped out of the room and followed him, calling him back. He was dressed quite well—a cap with ear flaps on his head, though his clothes were getting shabby—and he begged me urgently to give him food. He was pleading, not for himself but for his mother who was too weak to move. If he could not get something for her to eat she would die, he said.

His urgency was irresistible. The prayer meeting had to go on without me. I beckoned to Mrs. Han and she slipped out, too. We got some food together and went back with the boy to see his mother.

She was lying on a ragged wadded quilt on the floor of a cart shed, and we learned that she and her husband and their little son had come from another district, even worse hit by the famine than Siangcheng. But her husband had died, she and the boy had had to fend for themselves, and now she was too ill to move. The boy had done what he could; gathered sticks and made a fire to try to warm her and then gone off to beg for food. He was desperate but determined. 'Bread! Bread! Give me bread!' His mother's life depended on him.

It is probably unnecessary to report that although many, many died in the famine, that boy and his mother came through it. We saw to that! Strangely enough, I can recall very little else about them. What I have always remembered was the urgency in that cry, so different from the unexpectant moaning of the beggars in the street. I have sometimes thought that much of our half-hearted praying is like the passionless pleas of those sighing beggars. It was the importunity in the cry of that boy that moved me to action. I think there must have been the same note in the voice of blind Bartimaeus that brought Jesus to a halt as He was passing through Jericho.

He is the God Who hears the cry.

22

Dear Edward,

It was just about the time the famine started that we received a letter which galvanised me, as missionary in charge in Siangcheng, to reluctant action. I had been feeling weary after six years in China without a proper holiday, and with no prospect of one in the foreseeable future. The Japanese had already attacked U.S. bases in the Pacific, bringing the States into the war against them, and many of our colleagues were now in Japanese internment camps. A furlough at home was out of the question with the Second World War raging in Europe. I remember one day thinking to myself:

'Well, I can keep going the way we are, just jogging along like this—but I couldn't rise to making a fresh effort.' We had a routine which, because of its regularity, had become undemanding. This letter challenged me to the very thing I had felt I could not do.

It came from Mission headquarters, which had been moved from the port of Shanghai on the east coast to the city of Chungking, a thousand miles inland to the west, which the retreating Chinese had made their wartime capital. The Mission Directorate was imparting to all of us who were scattered throughout free China a renewed vision of a truly indigenous church. This is what we should be aiming at getting established. Not a church in China that was dependent on western leadership and support, but a Church that was self-governing, self-propagating, and self-supporting: three Selfs.

(Even as I write these words I have to smile at the way the Communist Government has adapted to suit its own purposes the principle that had been clearly defined in missionary circles decades before. The name given to the state-controlled Church in China today is 'Three Self Patriotic Movement.')

There was nothing new in the idea. It was something that had been impressed on us right from the start of our missionary careers. The difficulty had been in its practical outworking. We were from the energetic West, we had come to live among the Chinese for the sole purpose of preaching to them the Gospel and teaching them to be disciples of Jesus Christ, and it was natural for us to go ahead and do it. When people were converted, and little groups of believers formed into churches, the missionary still instinctively took the lead and, often enough, the Chinese were content to follow. And since, in most cases, the people were poor, financial support for the work and for the provision of premises as places of worship were still coming largely from Mission sources.

The tendency with most of us missionaries was to accept the *status quo*, and the directive from

Chungking was designed to jerk us out of it.

'Evangelize—through the Church,' was the gist of its message, and it provided just the spark of inspiration needed to infuse new life into our task. Some of us had taken the admonition to leave church leadership to the Chinese so seriously that we were in danger of doing nothing at all, for fear of interfering. For me, the issue hadn't been difficult. As missionary in charge in Siangcheng, I had explained that I would devote myself to the women's work and occasional visits to the outstations, as I felt that church business and the leading of Sunday services should be in the hands of men, not women. I am afraid this apparently right-minded modesty was largely due to a natural disinclination for administration and public speaking. I was only too happy to leave such matters to the deacons and the resulting dichotomy between them and me might have continued to the end had it not been for the directive from Chungking.

This directive aimed at reassuring us missionaries that the vision of the evangelisation of China, which had brought most of us to the country in the first place, had not been lost sight of in the emphasis on an indigenous church. The task must be continued but the time had come for it to be done not independently but with the local church as the vehicle. Our job was to inspire the churches with which we were working to take the initiative; and some practical suggestions were made as to how we could set about it.

Without those practical suggestions I, for one, would not have known where to begin, for the directive, as it affected me, meant not only inspiring the deacons with an increased sense of responsibility for evangelism, but also encouraging them to provide their own place of worship instead of meeting in premises rented by the Mission.

I wondered how they would react to the suggestions I had to put forward. Very apprehensively, I asked if we could have a committee meeting.

I need not have worried. Looking back, I marvel at the perfect timing of things for all of us in that little church in Siangcheng. We had gone through a lot together, what with the ever-present threat of a Japanese advance, the tensions of the guerilla occupation and the food shortage. The experiences were bringing home to us the uncertainty and impermanence of our earthly existence, and I think we were ready for the challenge to direct our energies in an new way towards establishing God's kingdom among men right where we were. At any rate, that first committee meeting was more encouraging than I had dared to hope, with the deacons nodding in agreement as I shared some of the contents of the directive from Chungking. Especially there was the inspiration of the formation of an organisation to link together all the C.I.M. churches in the province of Henan, for mutual help and encouragement and the provision of evangelists and Bible teaching. It was an organization within the Chinese churches, with Chinese—not missionary—leadership and this put them on their mettle. Rather like children who are discovering that they can walk and want to do so unaided, the deacons were quite eager to go ahead along the lines suggested, particularly in the matter of getting their own church building.

We arose from that committee meeting with a new sense of purpose and with a warmer feeling towards each other. We agreed that we must have another committee meeting—to discuss matters further and to pray. And so things got started. The more committee meetings we had, the fonder we got of each other; and the fonder we got of each other, the more committee meetings we had. At one time we seemed to be having them every other day. The warmth and enthusiasm was communicated to the church members and, through the hard days of the famine, money was given, often at great sacrifice, to the fund for a church building of their own.

The day came when Doris and I were invited to go along the street and see the property that was being bought. It was quite a small courtyard of low buildings on all four sides of it with the usual heavy wooden doors and glassless window frames. Only one building boasted a tiled roof; the others were merely thatched. One of these buildings was to be the church. It was to be made large enough to accommodate about a hundred people by the simple but somewhat risky expedient of carving two arches in the wall that helped to support the roof, thus making two rooms into one. Doris and I looked on rather dubiously as this was being done, fearful of a complete collapse of wall and roof, but no such catastrophe occurred, and the deacons were well satisfied with the result.

Meanwhile, the famine was coming to an end at last, with a good sweet potato crop and spring vegetables to tide us over till the grain was reaped.

Life returned more or less to normal. There were rumours that the Japanese were preparing for another advance, and one evening Dr. Wang, who had friends among the military officials, came to see us and warn us that this time it was likely to be permanent.

'Don't risk remaining here too long,' she said. 'But if you don't get away in time, you can come with me and my family. We shall go into the country. Where we go, you shall go. Where we sleep, you shall sleep. What we eat, you shall eat.' She spoke in her slow deliberate manner, and we were touched, for we knew she meant what she said.

We had a letter from Mission headquarters, too, explaining that it might be necessary for us to move to Chowkiakow, forty miles to the west, to avoid being cut off by a Japanese offensive. But we had no definite instructions to do so and we had lived with alarms for four years now. The more immediate matter of the removal of Mrs. Han and her daughter, along with all the church furnishings, to the new premises claimed our attention along with preparations for the very first Sunday service in the new church.

It was an historic event. Although the day dawned wet and windy, the place soon filled up with men and women who looked around the freshly mudded walls with a kind of proprietary interest. In some ways the place compared unfavourably with the old one for it was much smaller and more congested. But it was their own, bought with their own money at the height of the famine; and, as I stood with a little group of them that

Sunday morning, I knew the Lord was there.

It was without any premonition of threatening clouds that I turned as someone spoke my name, and found Deacon Liong standing beside me.

'Teacher Dong,' he said in a low, but very clear voice. 'Here is a telegram for you.' He looked down at me impassively, but there was something about his manner that arrested me. Telegrams were rare, and as he held this one in his hand he asked, 'Shall I read it to you?' He knew I would have difficulty in deciphering the hasty scrawl. 'Yes, please.' I said. Again in that low, clear voice, he read to me the message it contained.

'Situation serious. Proceed with baggage to Chowkiakow immediately.'

I ought not to have been unprepared, for we had had those warnings; but, all the same, it came as a shock. I stood quite still for a moment, then said quietly, 'I'd been afraid of this.'

A man standing by asked anxiously what it meant, and quickly I murmured, 'Don't say anything.' That this should happen on the very first Sunday when the service was to be held on the new church compound! 'We mustn't let anything disturb them—not today.' I turned back to the little group with whom I had been talking, and walked away with them into the chapel.

Deacon Liong turned away impassively, too. A year ago I would have thought he did not care but I knew him better now. There was a wordless understanding between us to avoid any emotional demonstration of distress or alarm to spoil the joy of this day. All the same, as I sat among the women in the back rows, I found it no easy matter to control the conflicting thoughts of my mind and listen to the sermon. There would be so much work to do, and I wondered how soon 'immediately' could be.

After the service there was, of course, a committee meeting. Still I remained silent about the telegram. Not until various comments had been made about the arrangements for the service, and plans outlined for the future, did Deacon Liong look across at me and ask if I had anything to say, adding quietly, 'You'd better tell them your news, Teacher.'

So I told them. Teacher Way and I had received instructions to evacuate Siangcheng immediately, for fear of a Japanese advance that would cut us off; but we had been instructed to go to Chowkiakow, only forty miles away. Deacon Liong added reassuringly that there had been these rumours before; the teachers would probably be back again in two or three weeks' time, he said.

But as I went to bed that night, it was with the conviction that tomorrow would see the end of my service in Siangcheng. The thought was solemnizing. The books on this part of my life were closing. It would only remain, on the Day when they were opened, to give an account of what had been committed to me.

23

Dear Edward,

I don't know how to condense into a thousand
or two words what filled a book forty years ago
when I wrote about our last day in Siangcheng.
Everything had to be cleared, the premises
emptied, our stuff disposed of except what
personal possessions we could get onto a couple of
wheelbarrows or strap on the carriers of our
bicycles. But all that was incidental. What really
mattered, what filled the day, was the people: the
people who came to do what they could to help and
to say goodbye; the people with whom our lives
had been so closely interwoven for years, and who,
we realized, we would never see again.

It started with Deacon Hsiao's arrival. Alert and
capable, he attended to the Famine Relief grain. It
must all be distributed before we left, and I turned
instinctively to him for that. Firmly putting aside
his own affairs, he was in and out of the compound
most of the day, making lists of the neediest
people, weighing the grain, distributing it. He was
unusually quiet, and when he had finished he came
and said, 'I'm going back now, Teacher. If there's
anything else I can do for you, send over at once. I

shall not be far away.' We looked at each other silently then, for we knew it was goodbye. I wished I could think of some last word for him. Pastor Gee and Pastor Fee, the missionaries before me, had both given him the text—'Be thou faithful unto death, and I will give thee the crown of life'—as they were leaving. It had made a deep impression on him. But I seemed tongue-tied. Perhaps after the four years of our fellowship in the Gospel there was no need for further words.

'Thank you,' I said. He bowed and went away.

Then there was Mrs. Deng who hawked needles and other odds and ends to keep herself and her child alive, and had occasionally sold things for me or Doris when our funds were low. She came along for that purpose now; strong, reliable, ready to raise what money she could to provide for the uncertainties of the journeys that lay ahead of us. Picture frames, ornaments, crockery, clothing; she'd pick them up and ask, 'How much do you want for this, Teacher?' and off she'd go, time and again, to return with the money.

'I'd have died in the famine if it hadn't been for that bowl of porridge each morning,' she told me more than once. 'There's nothing that can't be gone through. Look at what the Lord has brought me through!' Mrs Deng had no idea what she meant to us, that last day in Siangcheng.

Mrs. Hsaio had no idea, either. She had been one of the first to hear the news, her husband having told her after the committee meeting, and she had come round, eyes red with weeping, to whisper softly, 'Teacher! You're going away . . . Oh, I wish you could live *for ever* in Siangcheng!' That unusual display of emotion was strangely comforting. It is so soothing to be loved!

Mrs. Han expressed her love in a different way. During the day she had been as fully occupied as we were, sorting her things, preparing for her move to the two little rooms where she was to live with her daughter on the new church premises. But in the afternoon, she came through the gate into our compound with Widow Wang, as she had come so many times before, but this time it was for a final, private visit. As our eyes met, she broke into a wailing cry, such as I had only heard once before, at the funeral of her father-in-law. Doris hurried forward to lead her gently to a chair, murmuring words to soothe her but I stood with my head buried in my hands, unable to speak.

So the day passed. Arrangements had to be made for a hasty departure next day; decisions had to be made about what we could take and what we must either sell or give away; items of furniture were sold to neighbours who got wind of what was happening; and, through it all, there was a little stream of Christians who had heard the news and came to say goodbye: Ma Tzu Meng, a well educated young man from a wealthy family, and New Covenant, a robust peasant about his own age; Li *Tai-tai*, strangely subdued, with a little group of women from the Street of the Oil House, and some men from the South Road: a peanut seller, a stocking maker, an elderly scholar, and an official in the city workhouse; Blind Joy, the beggar-girl married to a blind man about three times her age; Deacon Fan, who helped Deacon Hsaio with the Famine Relief distribution; Deacon Liong who, seeing the completeness with which we were disposing of everything, said rather reproachfully, 'It looks as though you hope you won't return, Teacher Dong.' We were giving the lie to his reassuring comments about being back in three weeks.

'It's not that I *hope* I won't return—I *fear* I won't return,' I answered. For I knew it was the end.

A twelve year old schoolboy who had recently been baptized came too, and Mrs. Han's schoolgirl daughter slipped in after dark, without her mother. Last of all came Dr. Wang, and Doris and I sat down with her rather soberly, knowing we would never do so again. Our times of intimate fellowship had not been many, but occasionally the Manchurian doctor, an exile from the home of her youth, had come to spend an evening with us; and the quiet talks over the supper table, the reminiscences, the unemotional intimacy of those evenings, had bound us together in a way that only exiles can know.

'My heart is very sorrowful,' she said. 'I know you ought to go. I should be worried if you did not go, for the situation is really serious this time. But my heart is very sorrowful.' She drew some money from her pocket, laid it on the table.

'This is the money for some of your crockery that I have bought,' she said 'and here is a little—only a very little—to help towards your travelling expenses.' We talked together for a short while, then she rose to go and we went with her, holding aloft the flickering oil lamp to cast a dim light over the bricked paths, through the compound, through the church and along to the street door.

'When you have gone,' said Dr. Wang in her

quiet deliberate voice. 'I shall never come to this place again. Goodbye, Teachers. I shall not come to see you to-morrow morning.'

'No, Dr. Wang,' we said, 'Please do not come.' Then, the last words, the Christian farewell—'The Lord be with you.'

Dawn. Quick, last minute packing. Big Sister Lee foreseeing needs, hurrying to meet them. Deacon Hsaio arriving—were the Teachers ready for breakfast? He had insisted that he and his wife should supply it. Hasty distribution of bundles specially prepared for Mrs. Han, Widow Wang, and Big Sister Lee.

Arrival of New Covenant to see to the loading of the wheelbarrows and march alongside them all the way to Chowkiakow. Final instructions for the distribution of furniture and remaining possessions. The group of people who had come to say goodbye crowding into our little dining room and overflowing into the bedroom, for a last prayer together. Out into the little garden, all stamped down and forlorn-looking now. Never again would I see Sister Lee squatting under the shady acacia tree, preparing vegetables for the midday meal. Never again would I see the Bible class girls with their straight black bobbed hair, slim and dainty in their long gowns, wandering around looking at the flowers and smelling the roses. Never again would I see the men who came to the Sunday afternoon Bible class, filing slowly but purposefully into the little dining-room, their Bibles tucked under their arms . . .

'It's getting late—we must go . . .'

I had just crossed the threshold of the chapel in my hurried walk towards the street door, when time suddenly stood still. The benches had gone, the pulpit had gone, only a few posters, too torn to be worth removing, remained on the brick walls. All had been conveyed to the new church building. Never again would I see the blue-garbed throng of men and women gathered there for worship on Sunday morning, or sit with the little group that circled round in the centre of the hall to remember the Lord's death, when sometimes we had all but seen Him helplessly nailed to the cross, dying for us.

I had just crossed over the threshold in my hurried walk towards the front hall and the street door, when God spoke to me.

It was an experience I will never forget. I heard nothing, but I knew He was speaking, as my mind was flooded with one sentence which completely submerged all the busy thoughts and conflicting emotions of sorrow and excitement that had been filling it. Just as it had been flooded with verses about angels on that memorable day in Taikang, just as it had been flooded with the command not to resist when the brigand had broken into the out-station chapel at midnight, so a simple sentence from one of the parables in Matthew chapter 25 flooded my mind now. It was a word of commendation, the 'Well done' spoken to the servants who, when their master called on them to give account of the money he had entrusted to them, had traded profitably.

There was such grace in the words, such un-merited favour, as to bring tears to my eyes and halt me in my path. I stopped dead. It seemed too good to be true. In spite of all my failures and foolishness, in spite of my impatience and faithlessness, I'd made the grade. I felt like a student anxiously scanning the exam results who, wonder of wonders, sees his name on the pass list.

It would have been a relief to fling myself on my knees and give expression to my pent up feelings. But there was no place to obtain such privacy now and no time, either. The wheelbarrows had trundled off, Mrs. Han's daughter and Deacon Liong's son were waiting to push our bicycles out into the street and escort us down the familiar North Road with its avenue of old trees.

'Goodbye! Goodbye! The Lord be with you!' we called to our friends.

We passed through the north suburb with its stalls and inn benches. Mrs. Yen rose from her stool as she saw us coming and greeted us with the usual words, 'Where are you going, Teachers?'— adding with dismay, 'To Chowkiakow! Why? . . . Oh! I didn't know. No-one told me . . . You're going . . . Here, wait a minute!' Quickly she gathered up half-a-dozen round bread biscuits. She ran after us and thrust them into our hands, saying, 'Here, take these to eat on the way . . .' Standing there, looking at us, she reiterated, 'I didn't know, no-one told me you're going . . .'

Clear of the suburb at last, on the dusty track leading through the wheat-fields, we got off our bicycles, laid them down, sat on a mound by the side of the road, and buried our faces in our hands. Less than forty-eight hours earlier, we had been in the new church compound, completely unaware that we were so soon to be uprooted from the place and the people we had come to know so well. What lay ahead of us we did not know, but it was not so much the future that weighed on us, as the consciousness of those we were leaving behind.

'Lord! Bless them . . . Help them . . . Keep them . . . Thou art the good shepherd . . .'

After a while we got on our bicycles, and cycled away.

24

29 July 1987

Dear Edward,

Two and a half years have passed since we met in the Charing Cross Hotel and I told you I wouldn't write my own story. Well, as you will see, I have only covered a limited part of it, but this is how it seems to have come. In view of the reason for writing it at all, it probably deals with the most significant part. You may remember that when you broached the subject it was because of the China interest.

'There are so few people left who knew China before the Communists gained control,' you said.

Certainly, they had not gained control in the early 1940s. They had completed their Long March, and were entrenched in the northern mountains, biding their time; but when Doris and I cycled away from Siangcheng in 1943 we were scarcely aware of their existence. It was the wave of the Japanese armies spreading over all the areas where we Henan missionaries lived that had affected us. The journey to Chowkiakow was only the beginning of a much longer trek as we joined up with others and moved farther and farther westward. (It was at about this time that Glady's

Aylward was making her epic escape with all those children over the mountains, by the way. I met her not long afterwards, for the first time, in the city of Sian, where she told me of the way she had got to China across Russia and Siberia, and much more besides. This personal knowledge of her gave me confidence in writing *A London Sparrow* many years later).

I had been in touch with Mission authorities about going to the Tibetan border, and was told I could do so, but not until I had had a furlough. So I went to Mission headquarters in Chungking instead, where I got involved in editorial work before returning to England; by aeroplane to Calcutta, then by troopship to berth in the Clyde.

The tide of war was turning in favour of the Allies at last, and I remember listening in to the crossing of the Rhine and the final capitulation of Nazi Germany, and then to a most inspiring radio programme in which we heard the chimes of cathedral bells ringing out from all the liberated capitals of Europe.

That was followed, some time later, by the Victory Parade, as representatives of the armed services—the Navy, the Army, the Air Force, the Marines—went swinging down the Mall to take the salute as the King stood to acknowledge them. They were followed by a heterogeneous stream of others who had played their part, even risked their lives, in the dark days of the conflict—the medics, the nurses, the Red Cross, the Wrens and the WAAF, the Women's Voluntary Service and the air raid Wardens, and many more. The great moment for them all was when they came abreast of the

King and saw him standing there, saluting them—proud of them.

I listened in to that programme with deep emotion. The memory of it still stirs me. It seemed like a foreshadowing of the great Victory Parade when our King returns in glory. I want to be able to hold my head up in that Parade.

The dropping of the first atomic bomb on Hiroshima in August, 1945, not only marked the end of World War Two, as Japan surrendered unconditionally to the Allies, and ushered in a new era in world history as mankind entered the atomic age. It was also the signal for the Communists in North China to start moving.

By the time I got back to China, at the end of 1947, they were already overrunning the vast areas that the Japanese had occupied and any hope of missionaries returning to the province of Henan had to be abandoned. As for me, I set off for the Tibetan border, leaving Shanghai early one wet Monday morning in February, 1948, on the first lap of the journey. I travelled in a lorry containing three and a half tons of Bibles, one of a convoy of five vehicles—two lorries, two jeeps with trailers, and a saloon car. There were seven of us in the party—three Americans, two British, a Swede and a Chinese. We were bound for Chungking, 1,000 or so miles inland, and the month-long journey was sufficiently eventful what with hairpin bends and the lorry toppling over into the river to justify my writing another book: *Bible Convoy*.

And that was the last of my China experiences to appear in book form for a very long time. Although I travelled widely during the next three years—to Kangting on the Tibetan border, to Howhwan on a tributary of the Yangtze, to Lanchow on the upper reaches of the Yellow River, and to Ningsia on the border of Mongolia— nothing could be published about my travels, except in short articles in the Mission's magazine. The Communists were already established in Peking, the capital, and it was only a matter of time before they would be in control of the whole country. As citizens of the 'capitalist' nations of the West we were viewed with suspicion, even hostility, and we knew that anything appearing in print under our name could not only endanger our- selves, but also the Chinese with whom we were associated.

Even when the Mission drew out of China al- together, in 1951, our lips were sealed regarding what we had seen and heard. Our exit visas had been granted only on condition that Chinese friends resident in the country would stand guarantee for us. They, not we, would have to pay the price for anything detrimental to the Communists that we divulged. It was a most effec- tive way of keeping us quiet, and explains why I did not even write *The Reluctant Exodus*, the story of how the several hundred of us all got safely out of China, until nearly thirty years after it had happened.

So back to England I came—and the curtain went down on China. Occasional snippets of news got through—of arrests, imprisonments, execu- tions, the closing of churches and the persecution of Christians—but, as the years passed, a blanket of silence seemed to shroud the land. I was editing the

Mission's magazine by this time and, in an effort to maintain interest in the country, I ran a regular feature called 'Window on China', to which Leslie Lyall was the main contributor. It seemed all that I could do.

Then, one evening in 1970, I fell and fractured my arm and was taken to a local hospital. There I discovered, to my amazement, that practically all the trainee nurses were Chinese. True, they were from Malaysia, Singapore or Hong Kong, not from China, but there was no question about their race. Chinese girls, right on my doorstep! Had it not been for my fractured arm, I doubt whether I would have become aware of their existence. But, from that time on, I had a little stream of them coming to my terraced house in North London, to keep alive my love for the Chinese. Even where I am living now, in South-west London, I am within walking distance of the Chinese Overseas Christian Mission, founded in 1950 by a refugee from China, the Rev. Stephen Wang. Through the years, during which I have become absorbed in the writing of one book after another, China and the Chinese have been woven like a golden thread through the tapestry of my life. The monthly meeting for prayer for China that I attend is a *must* in my diary, and how I glow inwardly when the news from Henan is of spectacular church growth! There are more Christians in that one province now than there were in the whole of China when I left it in 1951!

It's time I finished this last letter and got it into the post to meet the publisher's deadline. I am aware that I ought to conclude on a picturesque or touching or challenging note. It would be very suitable, in view of what I have just written, if it were something about China, and I've been sitting quietly, letting my memory run back over my life, to see what comes to mind.

And what comes to mind just now is not China. As I grow older, I find that the most vivid experience, and the one that I remember most frequently, is the day in 1933, when I heard those words: 'Jesus Christ died on the cross to give you everlasting life, and all you've got to do is to accept it.' I never cease to marvel that it was as simple as that—and that it worked.

That was the day I started my pilgrimage. It will end when I see my master face to face.

ORDERING YOUR PRIVATE WORLD

Gordon MacDonald
Foreword by Selwyn Hughes

Every Christian has the opportunity to bring order
into his or her life—by inviting Christ to take full
control over each area.

*'This book struck me right between the eyes with conviction
and I wish that I had read it many years ago. Every
Christian leader ought to read this book.'*
　　　Billy Graham

HIGHLAND BOOKS

ISBN 0 946616 19 1

WHAT IS A FAMILY?

Edith Schaeffer

In an age when the family is being threatened as never before, Edith Schaeffer presents a powerful reaffirmation of the joys of family life. She writes as wife, mother and grandmother at L'Abri, the Christian community in Switzerland.

HIGHLAND BOOKS